"Thomas Schmidinger's second book on the Syrian Kurds and their place in the Syrian conflict focuses on the enclave of Afrin, which was recently occupied by Turkey and its Syrian proxies. One of the few scholars to have actually visited Afrin in recent years, Schmidinger provides a balanced account of the various religious and ethnic groups and political forces involved, of the way self-government was organized, and of the Turkish intervention. This is essential reading for anyone wishing to understand the current situation in northern Syria."
Martin van Bruinessen, Utrecht University

"Thomas Schmidinger's book provides a concise, clear, and remarkably comprehensive look at the history and contemporary politics surrounding Afrin. His work offers an invaluable primer, but even readers already well versed in the issues will find a wealth of new information. And those looking for an informative and probing analysis of the issues will not be disappointed."
David Romano, Missouri State University

"A late-breaking, thoughtful, political book that provides insight into the struggle of people in Western Kurdistan for survival, · dignity, and peace! This study of the social history of Afrin and of the local effects of a war waged by regional and global powers exemplifies what critical social science should be about."
Andrea Fischer-Tahir, University of Marburg

"Thomas Schmidinger, who visited Afrin in 2015, describes both the PYD administrative structures governing the region and the party's tense relationship with other Kurdish parties in Syria, providing a detailed overview of the politics, history, culture, and religion of a region that recently made international headlines."
Die Presse, Austria

T0152489

The Battle for the Mountain of the Kurds

KAIROS

In ancient Greek philosophy, *kairos* signifies the right time or the "moment of transition." We believe that we live in such a transitional period. The most important task of social science in time of transformation is to transform itself into a force of liberation. Kairos, an editorial imprint of the Anthropology and Social Change department housed in the California Institute of Integral Studies, publishes groundbreaking works in critical social sciences, including anthropology, sociology, geography, theory of education, political ecology, political theory, and history.

Series editor: Andrej Grubačić

Kairos books:

Practical Utopia: Strategies for a Desirable Society by Michael Albert

In, Against, and Beyond Capitalism: The San Francisco Lectures by John Holloway

Anthropocene or Capitalocene? Nature, History, and the Crisis of Capitalism edited by Jason W. Moore

Birth Work as Care Work: Stories from Activist Birth Communities by Alana Apfel

We Are the Crisis of Capital: A John Holloway Reader by John Holloway

Archive That, Comrade! Left Legacies and the Counter Culture of Remembrance by Phil Cohen

Beyond Crisis: After the Collapse of Institutional Hope in Greece, What? edited by John Holloway, Katerina Nasioka, and Panagiotis Doulos

Re-enchanting the World: Feminism and the Politics of the Commons by Silvia Federici

Occult Features of Anarchism: With Attention to the Conspiracy of Kings and the Conspiracy of the Peoples by Erica Lagalisse

Autonomy Is in Our Hearts: Zapatista Autonomous Government through the Lens of the Tsotsil Language by Dylan Eldredge Fitzwater

The Battle for the Mountain of the Kurds: Self-Determination and Ethnic Cleansing in the Afrin Region of Rojava by Thomas Schmidinger

The Battle for the Mountain of the Kurds

Self-Determination and Ethnic Cleansing in the Afrin Region of Rojava

Thomas Schmidinger

Translated by Michael Schiffmann

The Battle for the Mountain of the Kurds: Self-Determination and Ethnic Cleansing in the Afrin Region of Rojava
Thomas Schmidinger. Translated by Michael Schiffmann
© 2019 PM Press.

ISBN: 978-1-62963-651-1
Library of Congress Control Number: 2018948936

Cover by John Yates / www.stealworks.com
Interior design by briandesign
All photographs by the author

10 9 8 7 6 5 4 3 2 1

PM Press
PO Box 23912
Oakland, CA 94623
www.pmpress.org

Printed in the USA by the Employee Owners of Thomson-Shore in Dexter, Michigan.
www.thomsonshore.com

Contents

FOREWORD TO THE ENGLISH EDITION ix

PREFACE by Andrej Grubačić xi

INTRODUCTION xvii

Afrin and the "Mountain of the Kurds" 1

Population and Language 4

Religious Communities 7

History 22

Democratic Confederalism in the Canton of Afrin 49

Development of the Canton of Afrin from 2012 to 2018 64

Kurdish Enclaves in the Afrin Area 72

The War against Afrin 77

Voices from Afrin 113

What Next? 129

ACRONYM KEY 133

BIBLIOGRAPHY 135

INDEX 139

ABOUT THE AUTHORS 146

Foreword to the English Edition

Even though I'm extremely happy that this book has met with so much interest and that there is now an English translation, since the German first edition there have been quite a few ominous developments in the region.

Since the conquest of the city and region of Afrin by Turkey and its allies, the news has been very bad. There is no access whatsoever for independent media or scholars, which makes verifying news from Afrin extremely difficult. Nevertheless, I have done my best to update this history of Afrin and to give a brief description of the events that followed Turkey's conquest of the region. A book can never be totally up-to-date, but I wanted to at least touch on the direction events have taken since March 18, 2018. The goal of this book is not just to inform the international public about how much history and culture is being destroyed but also to jolt it awake and remind it of its responsibility to the people of and from Afrin. Now that more than two hundred thousand people have been expelled from Afrin, this is an increasingly pressing responsibility.

Vienna, November 1, 2018

The Battle for Afrin

Let me begin with a curious paradox. Reading mainstream press, academic monographs, and leftist reports on the Middle East leaves American readers with a distinct feeling of despair. Journalists speak of the absence of democracy and modern political forms. Yet, in the middle of this region, there is a political space known to Kurds as Rojava, where democracy has been developed to an almost unprecedented degree. One could argue that democratic confederalism in Rojava is actually a more developed form of democracy than systems of representative governance that are mistakenly referred to as democracy. However strange this inclusive system of council-based, bottom-up governing practices might appear to a well-educated academic, there is little doubt that direct democratic forms and cooperative techniques developed in the stateless democracy in Syrian Rojava are a politically and sociologically remarkable example of egalitarian politics. Orientalist scholars often remind us of the grim reality of the "clash of civilizations," with the Middle East serving as a paradigmatic case. However, the democratic federation of Rojava is home to a "democratic nation" developed to promote the peaceful coexistence of multiple ethnicities.

Humanitarian activists campaign tirelessly against the subjugation of women in the Middle East, but surprisingly there is a curious absence of reports on Rojava, whose constitution rests on three pillars: direct democracy, ecology, and liberation of women. A colleague from the Rojava University recently referred to women as the first colony. This is why any project of emancipation has to start with the history of male domination. In European press, there is an occasional mention of the remarkable courage of Kurdish women's militia, the YPJ, but these sensationalized accounts omit the existence of the refined body of thought commonly referred to as "jinology," a scholarly study of women's liberation in Mesopotamia.

Political theorists speak eloquently of post-fascism and neofascism, and everyone is understandably shocked by the gruesome violence of the Islamic State, but few mention the antifascist struggle waged by the Syrian Kurds and the international brigades of European volunteers. Leftist activists bemoan the political status quo and the absence of alternatives to the rising right-wing populism, yet in Kurdish Syria a genuinely revolutionary society is being built and improvised from below and developed and sustained in the incredibly challenging circumstances of war.

Lastly, ecologists and environmentalists who speak about the need for an environmental justice movement, of the urgent need to transform the state of "indecisive agitation" into a viable political project, are largely unaware of the social ecology of Kurdish Rojava and its intricate system of ecological councils, networks, and anti-extractivist projects.

How can we explain this paradox? Certainly, a lack of reliable information is one explanation. There is almost too much to pay attention to in the tragic recent history of Syria (and Turkey). However, I suspect that there is something else going on, as well. The silence and unease that is palpable in various comments about the Kurdish struggle have more to do with the nature of the Kurdish revolutionary project: a form of political and intellectual organization that stands in stark opposition to liberal certainties, orientalist prejudices, and leftist revolutionary designs. Perhaps the language of clash of civilizations is not entirely misplaced.

What is the philosophy behind the Rojava revolution and the new chapter in the Kurdish liberation project? We could describe it as a confrontation between two versions of modernity. The Kurdish liberation movement speaks of a "democratic modernity" that opposes "capitalist modernity." Democratic modernity as an integral organization of democratic nation, democratic communalism, and ecology. The cornerstone of this organization is a vision of a multiethnic nation detached from a dominant ethnicity. The defining element of democratic modernity, conceived of as an entirely different civilization, not just an alternative to the capitalist accumulation and the law of value, is one that requires a completely new definition of the concept of nation: as an organization of life detached from the state, a democratic nation as the "right of society to construct itself." It is a consociation based on free agreement and plural identity. As a democratic organization of collective life, it is not based on homeland and market but on freedom and solidarity. In opposition to nation-statism, the democratic nation detaches itself from the nation-state, a core institution of capitalist modernity.

The basic political format of a democratic nation is democratic confederalism with democratic autonomy; an expression of a democratic nation, conceptualized as a pluricultural model of communal self-governance and democratic socialism. Democracy is understood to be a practice and process of stateless self-governance: the power of horizontally networked communities to govern themselves. The Kurdish liberation movement opposes the idea of a territorially bounded nation-state and linear progress that defined the liberal utopia. Capitalist modernity was built on this peculiar cultural construct of a state of nature, with an assumed inevitability of progress that blurred imperialism/colonialism abroad and representative democracy at home. Democratic modernity as a "collective expression of liberated life" stands in stark civilizational opposition to the capitalist trinity of patriarchal nation-state, capitalism, and industrialism.

This is the system that was, for all its shortcomings, implemented in the Afrin region, as detailed in this timely new book. Thomas Schmidinger, one of the few genuine experts on the topic of Kurdish politics, exposes many of the contradictions of a democratic autonomy under construction, while all the same remaining cautiously optimistic about its successful implementation. While Afrin was not a model of an ideal revolutionary society, it certainly contained a germ of a stateless democracy within the context of a democratic autonomy. This well-organized and illuminating account of the Afrin war includes an authoritative history of the region known as the "Mountain of the Kurds." As far as I am aware, this is the first book in English on the topic of Turkish invasion against the Rojava Kurds. However, the timing is far from its only contribution. Schmidinger gives a comprehensive and objective account of the events that transformed this "island of peace" and multiethnic "mini-Syria" into an occupied territory emptied of its residents. The book artfully combines interviews and documentary material (in my opinion, the most valuable part of the book), relevant secondary accounts, and shrewd analysis that maintains a delicate balance between condemnation of Turkey and the European Union and of the "romantic dreams of European coffeehouse revolutionaries." The result is rigorous and competent book by a scholar and activist in critical solidarity with the Kurdish liberation project. This critical position allowed the author to focus on his immediate task: a documented analysis of the Turkish offensive against Afrin and the Mountain of Kurds.

On March 6, 2018, the Turkish troops and their jihadi allies began their advance toward Afrin. Beginning on March 10, Turkish forces bombarded the homes of civilians, who at that point were resisting leaving the besieged town. Interviews with the civilians led the author to conclude that the Kurdish defense units known as the YPG and YPJ did not prevent civilians from leaving the town. The bloodiest day of the invasion was certainly March 16, when indiscriminate bombardment took the lives of at least forty-seven civilians, including the wounded in the Afrin hospital. The YPG and YPJ speedily withdrew from the city on March 18. Although he presents a number of possible explanations for this surprising move, the author believes that the real aim was to enable the safe retreat of the civilians. He maintains that the decision to withdraw from the city "probably did prevent an even worse bloodbath, while allowing the refugees to flee."

The relatively stable border between the YPG/YPJ and the Turkish army (and its jihadist allies) reemerged on April of 2018. The entire Kurdish region of Afrin, with some exceptions in the east of the city, is now under the Turkish occupation. In these occupied areas, plundering and violence, including forced conversions of civilians, is taking place, although exact figures are impossible to ascertain. The United Nations estimates that up to seventy thousand civilians remain in Afrin, which is occupied by Islamist militias that enforce strict dress codes, while saluting the Turkish flag and decorating the schools in the region with pictures of Erdogan.

Why did the Turkish regime invade Afrin? The author suggests three principal reasons: destruction of the project of democratic autonomy, ethnic cleansing of the Kurdish population, and the EU-sponsored relocation of refugees from Syria. This plan is premised on the conscious and calculated intention of mobilizing "future ethnic conflicts."

The greatest contribution of this excellent book is arguably the careful and detailed exposure of European complicity in the Turkish operations against Afrin. To give but one example, the German state has not ceased to export military equipment, including combat tanks, to Turkey (as high as 4.4 million pounds during the first weeks of the war; 98 million pounds in 2016). Exporting conflict goes hand in hand with importing Turkish politics and cracking down on Kurdish protests. Kurdish demonstrations are prohibited in Germany, home to a large Kurdish population, in an alleged effort to prevent the "importation of the conflict."

To be sure, the most important part of the German and European assistance to the Turkish army resides in the European refugee policy. As the author makes clear, the cornerstone of the so-called refugee deal was the Action Plan for the Limitation of Immigration via Turkey, and later, in 2016, the new EU-Turkey agreement. Under the provisions of this document, Turkey will receive almost six billion euros to keep the refugees in Turkey, far away from Europe. As European authorities were undoubtedly aware, almost four million additional people in Turkey was bound to create a host of social and economic problems for Turkey itself. This contributed to Turkey's decision to conquer Afrin: "In doing so the Turkish regime is not just concerned with domestic political power objectives and the destruction of de facto Kurdish autonomy but also with the repatriation of the refugees to Syria." This anti-refugee policy, which amounts to "erecting a defense wall against refugees," should resonate with those American readers concerned with Donald Trump's xenophobic, authoritarian populism.

Repatriation and the "readmission of refugees" was one of the many propaganda lies of this terrible war. As Thomas Schmidinger makes abundantly clear, there were no refugees from Afrin in Turkey. The narrative was as consistent as it was false: allegedly Afrin was home to an Arab majority and a Turkmen minority, with Kurds making up only 35 percent of the population. The predictable result of the war is ethnic cleansing. Turkish forces, aided by their jihadist allies, have successfully expelled the civilian population, "creating room for the Turkish government resettlement program." Giving the land "back to its rightful owners," another oft-repeated propaganda slogan, in reality means Arabization and Turkmenization of the region and the destruction of its Kurdish character. Turkish NATO partners and Russia are united in tacit approval of this genocide. The much-vaunted "return of refugees" basically meant filling the houses of expelled civilians with Arab and Turkmen settlers from East Ghouta, as part of a larger project of Arabization and Turkmenization of the region. As I write this preface, more than two hundred thousand people have been expelled from Afrin.

This competent book is a welcome introduction to the history of Afrin. It is conceived of as a research tool, a compass to help us both to navigate the labyrinth of information about bellicose Turkish politics in the region and to illuminate the contradictions inherent in the Kurdish revolutionary project. More specifically, the book seeks to bring to light the obscured events of the Afrin war, as well as the contradictions of a moment that marked a historical turning point for people in the Afrin region.

Andrej Grubačić

Introduction

When I visited the autonomous canton of Afrin in 2015, what I found was a truly beautiful landscape and a tranquil people who, even though they were living under difficult conditions, were finding a way to live and were above all pleased to have overcome the dictatorship of the Arab nationalists, at least for the time being. The hopes of the ordinary people were not always as far-reaching as those of the political functionaries. Many of them just wanted a peaceful life alongside their Arab and Turkish neighbors.

That compared to the other regions of Syria Afrin was an island of peace was made clear by the fact that people from all over Syria had sought and found refuge there. Afrin became a sort of mini-Syria. It is not that there weren't any conflicts or political problems. Afrin was no idyll, and I cherish the region too much to take the opportunity to project the romantic dreams of European coffeehouse revolutionaries onto it. But the people of the Kurd Dagh, the "Mountain of the Kurds," as this region has been called for centuries, deserve a peaceful future, a future that the Turkish military attack that began on January 20, 2018, is meant to destroy.

The task of this book is to tell their story, to arouse its readers, and to make at least a small contribution to opposing the injustice done to the people there while I was writing this book and the Austrian publisher of the German edition was working as quickly as possible to publish it. Even though this book is based on a very long familiarity with and involvement in the region, it is, nonetheless, a "quick shot," in the sense that I wrote it in just a few weeks, and the publisher got it onto the market very shortly thereafter. The price of working at that pace is that this book can only be rudimentary. It tells a story of the region but certainly also omits many facts and anecdotes that would have enriched the narrative.

Since the beginning of 2017, I have been trying to return to Afrin for further field research, but since 2015, shortly after my first stretch of field research, the path through A'zaz (which had already been difficult enough to traverse) has been ruled by various Islamist groups and has become just as impenetrable as the green border, which Turkey had turned into an imposing barrier. My only option would be to travel through government areas, but I have never acquired the necessary visa. As a result, I have been limited to communicating from far afield with acquaintances, friends, and political functionaries in the region, thus following events in Afrin from a distance. I have incorporated whatever I was able to take in through that process into this book to the best of my ability. I hope that the result will provide readers who haven't visited the region with an impression of what is being destroyed at this very moment.

As I was finishing this book, hundreds of thousands of civilians were fleeing from Afrin. At this point, the international community, which allowed this massacre to unfold and, in part, even enabled it through its arms deliveries to Turkey, bears a lasting responsibility. Despite its conquest by the Turkish army and the Islamist militia allied with it, the history of Afrin is not yet at an end. It is, of course, incumbent upon the readers of this book to remind their own states of their responsibilities.

Vienna, March 18, 2018

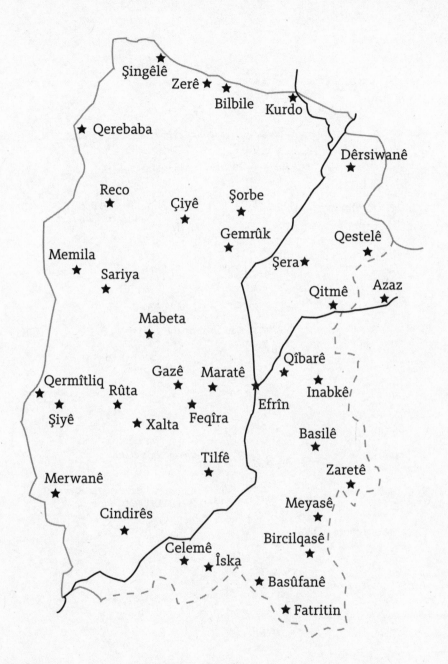

Şingêlê
Zerê
Bilbile
Kurdo
Qerebaba
Dêrsiwanê
Reco
Çiyê
Şorbe
Gemrûk
Qestelê
Memila
Şera
Sariya
Qitmê
Azaz
Mabeta
Qîbarê
Gazê
Maratê
Inabkê
Qermîtliq
Rûta
Efrîn
Şiyê
Xalta
Feqîra
Basilê
Tilfê
Zaretê
Merwanê
Meyasê
Cindirês
Bircilqasê
Celemê
Îska
Basûfanê
Fatritin

Afrin

TURKEY

Bilbile
Reco
Şera
Mabeta   Qitme   Azaz
Şiyê   Efrîn   Dabiq
Mara
Tal Rifaat
Cindirês   Nubl
Basûfanê   al-Zahraa
Atmeh   Anadan
Dar Taizzah   Qabtan al-Jabal   YPG
al-Dana   Aleppo

YPG/SDF

Islamic State

Jabhat al-Nusra

Syrian Regime/SAA

Islamic Front, Ahrar ash-Sham and
Nour al-Din Zenki Brigades

Afrin, January 2016

TURKEY

Bilbile

Reco

Şera

Qitme ★ Azaz

Mabeta

Şiyê ★ Efrîn ★ Dabiq
★ Mara

Tal Rifaat

Cindirês

Nubl
Basûfanê
al-Zahraa

Atmeh Anadan

Dar Taizzah
Qabtan al-Jabal YPG

al-Dana Aleppo

	YPG/SDF		Syrian Regime/SAA
	Turkey-backed "FSA"/Syrian National Army (from May 2017) SNA		Ahrar ash-Sham and Nour al-Din Zenki Brigades
	Haiat Tahrir al-Scham		

Afrin, Spring 2017

TURKEY

Bilbile

Reco

Şera

Mabeta   Qitme   Azaz

Şiyê   Efrîn   Dabiq
Mara

Tal Rifaat

Cindirês

Nubl
Basûfanê   al-Zahraa

Atmeh   Anadan

Dar Taizzah   Qabtan al-Jabal   YPG
al-Dana   Aleppo

YPG/SDF

Syrian Regime/SAA

Turkish army and Turkish-backed
"FSA"/ Syrian National Army
(from May 2017) SNA

Ahrar ash-Sham and
Nour al-Din Zenki Brigades

Haiat Tahrir al-Scham

Afrin, November 2017

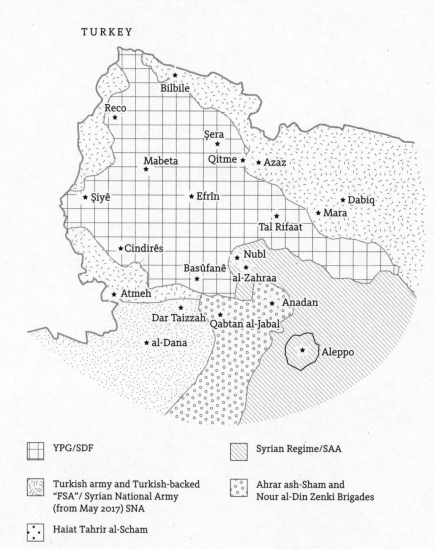

TURKEY

Bilbilê
Reco
Şera
Mabeta   Qitme ★ Azaz
Şiyê   ★ Efrîn   ★ Dabiq
                        ★ Mara
                Tal Rifaat
Cindirês
            Nubl
      Basûfanê ★
            al-Zahraa
Atmeh   Anadan
      Dar Taizzah
         Qabtan al-Jabal
      al-Dana   ★ Aleppo

	YPG/SDF			Syrian Regime/SAA

Turkish army and Turkish-backed
"FSA"/ Syrian National Army
(from May 2017) SNA

Ahrar ash-Sham and
Nour al-Din Zenki Brigades

Haiat Tahrir al-Scham

Afrin, February 2018

Afrin and the "Mountain of the Kurds"

The region of Afrin in the northwest of Syria is also called Kurd Dagh, an older Ottoman name meaning "Mountain of the Kurds." It is also used in Arabic (Ǧabal al-Ākrād) and Kurdish (Çiyayê Kurmênc in the local dialect). In Turkish, Kurd Dagh was distorted into Kurt Dağı in order to turn the "Mountain of the Kurds" into the Mountain of the Wolves (Kurt). Next to the Ǧabal al-Anṣārīya (Mountain of the Nusayrians) and the Ǧabal ad-Durūz (Mountain of the Druze), the Ǧabal al-Ākrād is one of the three "ethnic mountain regions" of Syria where minorities had settled and, in part, retreated: the Druze religious minorities on the Ǧabal ad-Durūz, the Alevi, who are also called Nusayrians, on the Ǧabal al-Anṣārīya, and, of course, the Kurdish ethnic minority on the Ǧabal al-Ākrād.

Until the partition of the Ottoman Empire after World War I, the northern areas that are today under Turkish rule were also regarded as a part of the Kurd Dagh. In Syria, the southern and central part of the "Mountain of the Kurds" became the region of Afrin. Qermîleq, the most western village in the region, directly at the border with Turkey, is only thirty-eight kilometers [twenty-three and a half miles][1] away from the Mediterranean Sea. Until the Turkish annexation of the Antakya/Hatay region between Afrin and the Mediterranean in 1938–1939, these villages in the west were more oriented toward Antakya and the Mediterranean ports than toward Aleppo. The larger part of the region, however, belonged to the sphere of influence of the Kurdish town of Kilis, which

---

1   This and all subsequent conversions are close approximates.

The region of Afrin (Kurdish: Efrîn) is known for its olive orchards, said to contain a total of twenty-three million trees. Fruit and vegetables are also grown in the villages of this soft hilly landscape.

today is part of Turkey, and from which the "Mountain of the Kurds" was cut off when the new borders were demarcated after World War I.

Altogether, the region comprises about 2,050 square kilometers [1,275 square miles]. Even though the whole Kurdish-speaking region around today's city of Afrin is frequently called Kurd Dagh, the Kurd Dagh in the narrower geographical sense is actually only the massif in the west and the northwest of the region that extends into Turkish territory on both sides. This Kurd Dagh is a low mountain range with many gentle hills that rise to between 700 to 1,200 meters [2,300 to 3,900 feet] above the sea level. The actual Kurd Dagh, the high plateau of the Ğabal Simʿān (Kurdish: Çiyayê Lêlûn) in the southeast that rises up to 876 meters [2,874 feet] and the Ğabal Barsa further to the north that is 848 meters [2,782 feet] high, encompasses the fertile plain of the Afrin River, a plain called Cûmê in Kurdish. This plain borders the 149 kilometer [93 mile] Afrin River, which issues into the Orontes (Arabic: Nahr al-Asi), in the Turkish province of Hatay. This river irrigates a plain that is the site of intense agricultural use, with the town of Afrin, which was built in the 1920s, at its northern end.

The hills of the actual Kurd Dagh have also been used agriculturally for thousands of years. Even though the climate is generally dry, the winter rain, which reaches an average volume of more than sixty mm [two and a half inches] in December and January, allows for the growth of fruit and vegetables.

But by far the most important agricultural product of Afrin is olives. The whole region is planted with millions of olive trees, some of which date back to the time of the Romans and testify to the fact that growing olives already characterized the region two thousand years ago. The high-quality olives and olive oil from Afrin were famous across the Levant and were the most important ingredient in the famous Aleppo soap.

Until the Turkish attack in January 2018, Afrin was one of the quietest regions in Syria. Up until then, the self-administration established in 2012 had succeeded in keeping the civil war away from the local population. Therefore, Afrin also became a haven for those expelled from other parts of Syria. But now, Afrin and the "Mountain of the Kurds" are in danger of being destroyed by the war. Already there are strong hints that Turkey and its allies not only want to occupy the region but also hope to expel the local population and settle Arab refugees from Syria there to enhance their control and create a buffer zone for Turkey.

Population and Language

Serious up-to-date data on the population of Afrin are impossible to get. Therefore, we can only guess that at the beginning of the Syrian civil war, three hundred to four hundred thousand people lived in the Afrin (Kurdish: Efrîn) region, of whom more than 98 percent had Kurdish as their mother tongue.

Since the Middle Ages at least, but possibly also in pre-Christian times, the region was characterized by Kurdish tribes (Kurdish: *Eşiret*) and by the beginning of the French protectorate was regarded as a coherent Kurdish settlement area. The Kurd Dagh was inhabited by five different Eşiret: the Amikan, Biyan, Sheikan, Shikakan, and Cums. The smaller tribes of the Robariya, Kharzan, and Kastiyan, among whom the Muslim Robariya exerted a kind of protectorate over the villages of the Êzîdî in the region, were much weaker.[1] Since the latter also spoke Kurdish, we can safely assume that almost the entire population was Kurdish-speaking by the beginning of the twentieth century. Thus, Afrin formed a region that was both ethnically and linguistically far more homogeneous than, for example, the Kurdish-dominated regions further to the east, where there were large Armenian minorities in the cities, where Aramaic-speaking regions alternated with Kurdish regions, and where Arab tribes had already been living before the Syrian regime's deliberate settlement of Arabs. Apart from the small Armenian community and the small number of Arabs from the Emirati and Bobeni tribes, there was scarcely any other group present.

---

1   Thomas Schmidinger, *Krieg und Revolution in Syrisch-Kurdistan: Analysen und Stimmen aus Rojava* (Vienna: Mandelbaum Verlag, 2014), 50.

The Dūmī, however, are one small minority that is still present in the region. They are related to the European Roma and occupy a position in the Middle East similar to that of the Roma in Europe. Most Dūmī still speak their own language, Domari or Nawari, as well as at least one or two other languages, usually Kurdish and Arabic. The Dūmī of Afrin as a rule also speak Kurdish. Because of cultural and social similarities, they are often regarded as a subgroup or "branch" of the Roma.[2] Some linguists, however, advance the thesis of an earlier autonomous migration of the Dūmī from India to the Middle East and trace the relationship of the languages back to earlier commonalities in India.[3] Alongside Turkish and Arabic loanwords, we also find Kurdish loanwords in the Dūmī language,[4] which is evidence of a long cohabitation with the speakers of these languages in the region.

Apart from their own language, the Dūmī of Afrin generally use Arabic or Kurdish. Since most of them have never had any official education, they are only rarely able to read or write these languages. The civil war has made the migrations of this group much harder. Since 2012, many of them have become semi-sedentary inhabitants of squalid huts or tents at the outer limits of Kurdish cities.

The Büd, a Kurdish-speaking group that came to Afrin from Besni, near Adıyaman (Kurdish: Semsûr) in today's Turkey, after the Sheikh Said uprising in 1925, have a similar status. The group refers to itself as "nomadic" (Kurdish: *Koçer*) but is referred to by outsiders as either Büd or Ghorbat (Kurdish for "gypsies"). Until recently, this group still lived in tents and wandered from village to village within the Kurd Dagh region, often crossing the Syrian-Turkish border in the process. In an interview with Kamal Sido of the Society for Threatened Peoples, a Büd woman explained: "For many years, we have regularly crossed the Syrian-Turkish border. For us, this border simply doesn't exist, and therefore, many of us speak Turkish really well."[5] The members of the group speak their own

---

2 Schmidinger, *Krieg und Revolution in Syrisch*-Kurdistan, 28.
3 Yaron Matras, *A Grammar of Domari* (Berlin: Walter de Gruyter GMBH & Co., 2012), 20 ff.
4 Yaron Matras, "Grammatical Borrowing in Domari," in *Grammatical Borrowing in Cross-Linguistic Perspective*, ed. Yaron Matras and Jeanette Sakel (Berlin: Walter de Gruyter GMBH & Co., 2007), 162.
5 Ayub Mustafa Shaeikho in an interview with Kamal Sido, February 18, 2015.

dialect and marry primarily among themselves. Many of them previously worked as basket makers and wandering dentists.

The number of Kurds living in the region at the beginning of the civil war can only be estimated but couldn't have been higher than four hundred thousand. But by 2018 about two hundred to three hundred thousand people expelled from other parts of Syria had been added to the region's population. At the same time, tens of thousands of people fled to Europe. But still, one can safely say that in 2018, compared to the population at the beginning of the civil war, a significant number of additional people lived in the region of Afrin. Among the new inhabitants are Kurds from Aleppo and other parts of Syria, as well as Arabs and members of other population groups in the country. Altogether, the region comprises 366 villages and settlements. The only real urban center is the town of Afrin (Kurdish: Efrîn), which according to the 2001 census had 43,434 recognized inhabitants, a number that had approximately doubled by the start of the civil war. Together with the displaced persons living in the city, the population of Afrin may have grown to around one hundred thousand before the Turkish attack in 2018.

Apart from Afrin, there are a few additional small-town centers that are important as regional market cities, including Cindirês in the south, Mabeta in the center, and the cities of Reco and Şiyê in the west.

The Kurds of Afrin speak Kurmancî, which is the most widespread form of Kurdish, and which is also spoken in the rest of Syrian Kurdistan, in most parts of Turkish Kurdistan, and in the northern areas of Iraqi Kurdistan and Iranian Kurdistan. But Efrînî, the dialect of Afrin, has some peculiar features in its grammar and pronunciation.

To the south and to the east of Afrin, there are additional Kurdish settlements representing mixed-language enclaves, where Arabic and Turkmen, as Turkish is called in Syria, are also spoken. The small town Til Eren (Arabic: Tal Aran), with its 17,700 inhabitants, and the nearby town of Tal Hasil/Tal Hasel, about ten kilometers [six miles] to the southeast of Aleppo, also have Kurdish majorities, as do the Sheikh Maqsood (Kurdish: Şêxmeqsûd) urban quarter in Aleppo and a number of villages in the districts A'zaz, al-Bab, and Jarābulus.

Religious Communities

Muslims

Today the overwhelming majority of the Kurds in Afrin are Sunni Muslims, even though many of them only converted to Islam in the twentieth century and have Êzîdî roots. The Sunni Muslims of Afrin belong to the Ḥanafī school of law, or school of thought (*maḏhab*), which distinguishes them religiously from most other Kurds.

The majority of Sunni Kurds in Syria, Iraq, Turkey, and Iran belong to the Shafi'i school of law, or school of thought. Today, this doctrine of Sunni Islam, which can be traced back to Muḥammad ibn Idrīs aš-Šāfi'ī (776–820), is primarily present in Egypt, East Africa, the former South Yemen and Dhofar (Oman), Indonesia, Malaysia, and among the Sunni Kurds but not among Sunni Arabs in Syria or the Turks in Turkey. The prevalence of the Shafi'i school of law in Syria and Egypt goes back to Ṣalāḥ ad-Dīn Yūsuf bin Aiyūb ad-Dawīnī, the founder of the Ayyubid dynasty, who became famous in Europe as Saladin, liberated Jerusalem from the crusaders in 1187, and was himself a Shafi'i Kurd. While the Ottomans would later show a preference for the Ḥanafī school of law and help to bring about the latter's breakthrough in the Arab cities of Syria, many Kurdish tribes have remained Shafi'i to this day. But Afrin is located at the periphery of Kurdistan, in the far west of the Kurdish linguistic area. The region belongs to the narrower sphere of influence of the city of Aleppo. In the twentieth century, the tribes had already ceased to play an important role, and the late conversion of many Kurds from the Êzîdî religion to Islam thus took place under the influence of Ḥanafī Sunnis from Aleppo and not as a result of the pressure of Shafi'i Kurds. Regardless of the minutiae of these processes, the fact is that today the Kurds of Afrin are the only Ḥanafī Kurds in Syria.

As in many rural regions of Syria and Kurdistan, here too Sunni Islam is strongly influenced by Sufi brotherhoods and local cults of the saints. Thus, at the ancient archaeological site of Cyrrhus (Κύρρος), near the village Dêrsiwanê, a hexagonal Roman mausoleum from the third and fourth centuries after Christ is venerated as the Tomb of the Nani Huri (prophet Huri). The mausoleum is an important regional pilgrimage site connected to a fourteenth-century mosque and a group of trees where pilgrims hang pieces of cloth inscribed with their personal wishes. In addition, on the northern exterior wall of the mosque there are also a few shallow recesses into which pilgrims can insert small pebbles. If these remain in place, this is a sign that a wish connected with this act will be fulfilled without requiring any sacrifice in return. And finally, a protective handprint made from the blood of sacrificial animals (the Hand of Fatima) is left on the wall.[1]

But this is far from the only sanctuary frequented by local Muslims. Several tombs of saints that are simultaneously used as meeting places for Sufi brotherhoods (Zāwiya), such as the Zāwiya of Sheikh Rashid located a few kilometers [a couple of miles] northeast of the city of Afrin or that of Sheikh Mahmud Husayn (who only died in 2000), are important local pilgrim sites.

Besides the Sufi brotherhoods of the Naqshbandīya—or, rather, the Khalidi current of the Naqshbandīya going back to Mewlana Xalidê Kurdî/Mewlana Khâlid-i Baghdâdî[2]—and the Qādirīya, both of which are

---

1   Gerhard Fartacek, *Pilgerstätten in der syrischen Peripherie: Eine ethnologische Studie zur kognitiven Konstruktion sakraler Plätze und deren Praxisrelevanz* (Vienna: Verlag der Österreichischen Akademie der Wissenschaften, 2003), 133–37.

2   The Naqshibandi sheikh, who hailed from Şarezûr, near the Iraqi-Kurdish Silêmanî, is called Mewlana Xalidê Kurdî in Kurdish, while in Arabic his name is Mewlana Khâlid-i Baghdâdî because of his activities in Baghdad. Born a Kurd in 1779, he had already studied Shafi'i law in Kurdistan before finding his way to the Sufism of the Naqshbandīya after his study of theology (*kalam*) and during his travels to Mecca and India. Until his death in 1827, he taught in Baghdad and Damascus. Today this current of the Naqshbandīya is the strongest one in all of Kurdistan and has produced many personalities who have been important to the Kurdish national movement, including the Barzani family and the Syrian-Kurdish Sheikh Ahmad Khaznawi.

widespread in all of Kurdistan, the brotherhood of the Rifa'iyya is also popular in Afrin. Beginning in the fifteenth century, this Sufi brotherhood founded by Ahmad ibn 'Ali ar-Rifa'i during the twelfth century was replaced by the Qādirīya in most parts of Kurdistan. But in Afrin, the followers of the sheikh, who is buried near the Iraqi Tal Afar, are relatively numerous to this day.

The emergence of new groups of Sufis in Afrin is by no means only a matter of the past. In his field research in the region, the social and cultural anthropologist Paulo Pinto observed that the last decades saw the development of new Sufi communities that are not necessarily in the tradition of a particular Sufi brotherhood, but, rather, gather around some charismatic sheikh.[3] When the sheikh dies, his tomb becomes the center of the new community.

Êzîdî

The south and the east of Afrin form the largest contiguous settlement area of the Êzîdî (in English, Yezidis or Yazidis) in Syria. The Turkish historian Birgül Acıkıyıldız, who specializes in the Êzîdî and the Ottoman Empire, believes that the presence of the Êzîdî in the region dates back to the twelfth century.[4] On the other hand, in his investigations among the Êzîdî in Syria and Iraq in the 1930s, the French Orientalist and Kurdologist Roger Lescot arrived at the conclusion that the first Êzîdî only settled in the region of Afrin in the thirteenth century.[5]

We know for sure that there must have been a strong presence of the Êzîdî in today's region of Afrin by the fifteenth century, because the important Kurdish poet, prince, and historiographer Sharaf ud-Dīn Khān al-Bitlīsī mentions their presence in his classical source on Kurdish historiography the *Sharafnāma*, which first appeared in 1597.[6]

---

3   Paulo Pinto, "Kurdish Sufi Spaces of Rural-Urban: Connection in Northern Syria," Études Rurales 186 (2010): 151.
4   Birgül Acikiyildiz, *The Yezidis: The History of a Community, Culture and Religion* (London: I.B. Taurus & Co., 2010), 65.
5   Roger Lescot, *Enquête sur les Yézidis de Syrie et du Djebel Sindjar* (Beirut: Institut français de Damas, 1938), 205.
6   Sharaf Khan Bidlissi, *Chèref-nâmeh ou fastes de la nation kourde*, vol. 2, trans. François Bernard Charmoy (St. Petersburg: Commissionnaires de l'Académie impériale des sciences, 1875), 67–68.

In the past, the Êzîdî represented a distinctly larger part of the population of the region than today, but they were in a dependent relationship with the Muslim Kurdish tribes in the region. Thus, the inhabitants of the Êzîdî villages were subordinate to the Muslim tribe of the Robariya.[7]

The Êzîdî religion is an autonomous monotheist religion that draws from several Middle East religious sources. The Êzîdî believe in a God for whom they use the Kurdish word for "God," which is also used by Kurdish Muslims, Christians, and Jews, namely, Xwedê. This God, however, is very abstract and normally interacts with humans only via mediating angels, particularly the Peacock Angel (Kurdish: Tawûsê Melek).

The Êzîdî religion as we know it today was shaped by Islamic and possibly also Christian, Jewish, and Manichean influences on a Western Iranian religion. One controversial point is how to assess the relationship of the Êzîdî religion to other Iranian religious orientations, particularly to Zoroastrianism. Today Philip Kreyenbroek, who is probably the most renowned Iranist to focus on the Êzîdî religion, writes that research regarding the relationship between Êzîdism and both Zoroastrianism and Yarsanism (a current that is equally widespread in Kurdistan) indicates that even though Êzîdism and Yarsanism "are related to Zoroastrianism, they do not directly stem from it. Rather, important elements of this religion go back to a very old Western Iranian tradition that also played a role in the emergence of Roman Mithraism, which one could thus call 'proto-Mithraism.'"[8]

The persecution of the Êzîdî is based on a misunderstanding handed down through the centuries, according to which they are devil worshippers. Apart from God, this religion, which in its present form goes back to the Sufi-Sheikh Adī ibn Musāfir (Kurdish: Şêx Adî), who lived in the twelfth century and came from Lebanon, venerates the Peacock Angel, who is regarded as the first and most faithful angel of God. Because the Peacock Angel was particularly reverent in his faith in God, he also kept God's first commandment, namely, to venerate *nobody* but God. Therefore,

---

7   Jordi Tejel, *Syria's Kurds: History, Politics and Society* (London: Routledge, 2009), 9.
8   Philip G. Kreyenbroek,"Die Eziden, die Ahl-e Haqq und die Religion des Zarathustra," in *Im Transformationsprozess: Die Eziden und das Ezidentum gestern, heute, morgen: Beiträge der zweiten internationalen GEA-Konferenz vom 04. bis 05.10.2014 in Bielefeld*, ed. Gesellschaft Ezidischer AkademikerInnen (Berlin: VWB-Verlag, 2016), 32.

after God made Adam, Tawûsê Melek refused the order to prostrate himself before the newly created human being. He was thus tested by God and passed, a narrative that starkly contradicts the Christian and Islamic idea of hell, in which this angel was punished and then transformed into the devil. Unlike these two religions, the Êzîdî have no concept of hell as a place of eternal condemnation. For the Êzîdî, God is almighty to such an extent that there can be no second force that represents personified evil. Nonetheless, the similarity of the story of the Peacock Angel to that of the Islamic and the Christian devil, who refused to bow down before humans out of arrogance, was used for centuries to insinuate that the Êzîdî were "devil worshippers," an absurdity when you consider that this kind of personified evil doesn't even exist in the Êzîdî worldview.[9]

A further accusation Muslims have often leveled at the Êzîdî is that, as opposed to Jews, Christians, and Zoroastrians, they are not a religion of the book,[10] suggesting that this religious minority has no claim to the protection classical Islamic law affords to the "religions of the book." And, indeed, the Êzîdî religion could even be called anti-literate, given that the essence of the religion and its songs, the Qewel, are always handed down orally. Muslims who understand the Islamic tradition such that their tolerance is extended only to the religions of the book pose a genuine problem for the Êzîdî. In response, a myth has developed among many Êzîdî that a Holy Book of the Êzîdî, the Meshaf-1 Reş (the Black Book), actually exists but has disappeared.[11] During my field research in Syria, I was even approached by Êzîdî sheikhs who claimed that this book had been stolen by Austrians and was now in a museum in Vienna, and who asked me whether I could not take steps toward having the book returned to the Êzîdî. In reality, however, there is no such book in any Austrian museum or in the Austrian National Library.

The background of this myth is that in 1913 the Austrian Orientalist Maximilian Bittner published a book titled *The Holy Books of the Êzîdî or Devil Worshippers* with the Austrian Academy of the Sciences.[12] The

---

9   Thomas Schmidinger, *Krieg und Revolution in Syrisch-Kurdistan: Analysen und Stimmen aus Rojava* (Vienna: Mandelbaum Verlag, 2014), 32.

10   Eszter Spät, *The Yezidis* (London: Saqi, 2005), 25.

11   Ihsan Çetin, *Midyat'ta etnik gruplar: Kürtler, Mhalmiler (Araplar), Süryaniler, Yezidiler, Türkler, Becırmaniler (Seyyidler)* (Istanbul: Yaba Yayınları, 2007), 78.

12   Maximilian Bittner, *Die heiligen Bücher der Jesiden oder Teufelsanbeter* (Vienna: Alfred Hölder Verlag, 1913).

Afrin was home to the largest Êzîdî minority in Syria. This was the headquarters of the Êzîdî association in the city of Afrin.

authenticity of book, which is barely a hundred pages long and is based on writings that had been bought from local Christians, remains controversial to this day.[13] Be that as it may, among the Êzîdî of the Middle East, these writings could certainly not have had the importance that the Quran has for the Muslims or that the Bible has for Jews and Christians, since there are no original copies of this "Holy Scripture" extant. The longing for an authentic Holy Scripture reflects the wish to be accepted as a religion of the book by their Muslim neighbors and to acquire the protection that would follow from this.

Most of the Êzîdî villages in the region are located to the west and south of the city of Afrin. In the north, Qestelê and Qitmê are among the most important. To southwest of Afrin, there is another larger Êzîdî village, Feqîra. But the main area of settlement lies in the southeast of the Kurd Dagh, and includes the villages Beradê, Bircê Hêdrê, Basûfanê, and Kîmarê.

---

13 Christine Allison,"'Unbelievable Slowness of Mind': Yezidi Studies, from Nineteenth to Twenty-First Century," *Journal of Kurdish Studies* 6 (2008): 12.

This is one of the reasons for the particularly difficult situation of the Êzîdî, whose villages became a target of attack for the Jabhat al-Nusra in 2012 and for the Hai'at Tahrir ash-Sham since 2017. In the north, most Êzîdî villages are located between the town of Afrin and the town of A'zaz, which was conquered by the Islamic State, Jabhat al-Nusra, and other opposition groups on September 18, 2013. This frequently places the approximately twenty Êzîdî villages in the region (the exact number depends on the counting method) directly at the front line of rival Arab and jihadist opposition groups.

Until 2018, the Êzîdî had been safe in the regions of Afrin under the control of the Kurds, but in the neighboring regions under the rule of pro-Turkish militia the picture has been quite different. On June 12, 2017, the Êzîdî inhabitants of the small village Elî Qîno in the northwest of A'zar were expelled. The village is located to the west of the barricade that the Yekîneyên Parastina Gel/Yekîneyên Parastina Jin (YPG/YPJ) had erected at the border of the area under their control and was under the de facto control of pro-Turkish rebels. On that day, a Monday, the Êzîdî population was given one hour to leave their homes. Most of the inhabitants fled to Afrin, and their houses were confiscated by pro-Turkish rebels.[14]

In today's Syria, this minority is under enormous pressure, but it also suffers as a result of the internal conflict between a current close to the Partiya Karkerên Kurdistanê/Partiya Yekîtîya Demokrat (PKK/PYD)[15] that is not only trying to reconfigure the Êzîdî religion as a variety of Zoroastrianism but also to reform it and the traditional Êzîdî who regard this very "Zoroastrianization" as an attack on their religion. Extremely strict marriage rules and the rigid social system, both of which are no longer accepted by some of the younger Êzîdî, are also a source of conflict.

Êzîdî society is divided into three groups that each have different social and religious functions: the simple faithful, the Murid, are only allowed to marry other simple faithful people; members of the Sheikh group, only other members their group; and the priests, or Pîr, only other

---

14 Thomas Schmidinger, "Militärische Expansion mit US-Unterstützung: Aktuelle Entwicklungen in Syrisch-Kurdistan," in *Wiener Jahrbuch für Kurdische Studien 5: Sprache—Migration—Zusammenhalt: Kurdisch und seine Diaspora*, ed. Katharina Brizić et al. (Vienna: Praesens Verlag, 2017), 239.

15 PKK: Workers' Party of Kurdistan, a party founded in Turkey under the leadership of Abdullah Öcalan. PYD: Democratic Union Party, founded as the sister party of the PKK in 2003; in 2012, it took control of the Kurdish areas in Syria.

Pîr. Among the older Êzîdî, the strict marriage rules that only allow for marriage within one's own group are still unquestioned. When I asked about this, an older member of the Pîr group from the village of Feqîra responded: "This is not open to debate. The marriage rules are a central part of our identity. All Êzîdî must stick to them."[16]

The religious identity crisis of many Êzîdî also has to do with the fact that the Êzîdî, particularly those of the Kurd Dagh region, have extremely limited access to the Êzîdî religious centers in today's Iraq, have few religious scholars, and, unlike the Êzîdî in the Ğabal Sinjar (Kurdish: Şingal) or in the Şexan region near their religious shrine in Lalish (LALiş), have been much more thoroughly integrated into the Sunni population. In the 1930s, Lescot described the Êzîdî in the Kurd Dagh region as a group that was hardly distinguishable from its compatriots.[17] The orientation of these Êzîdî toward a form of Êzîdîsm that the PKK has declared to be a variety of Zoroastrianism is also based on this far-reaching loss of old religious customs. In a way, it is the reinvention or new invention of a religion whose members in the Kurd Dagh, even though they still form a separate group, have for the most part already forgotten their religious traditions. Distinct from other regions of Kurdistan, the Êzîdî in Afrin were called Zawaştrî, that is Zoroastrians, even before the ascension of the PYD to power, although Zoroaster and his teachings actually didn't play a significant role at the time.

The form of the Êzîdî shrines (Ziyaret) in Afrin is different from that of the shrines in their religious centers in Iraq. The shrines are not characterized by the typical pointed conical roofs but are either simple flat-roofed buildings or are adorned with a cupola. For example, the Malak Adî shrine, which possibly refers back to Şêx Adî from LALiş, like many Islamic tombs in the region, only has a dome. The same is true for the shrine of Sheikh Barakat and other important Ziyaret. Only some of the newer Ziyaret have the pointed conical rooves typical for the Êzîdî in Iraq.

Unlike many other religious minorities in Syria, the Êzîdî have never been an officially recognized religious community. Even though the secular authoritarian Ba'ath regime has occasionally offered protection to Christians, Druze, or Alawi, it has not done so for the Êzîdî. It was only after the withdrawal of the Syrian regime from the Kurdish areas that

---

16 Pîr Majid in an interview with Thomas Schmidinger in Feqîra, February 2, 2015.
17 Lescot, *Enquête sur les Yézidis de Syrie et du Djebel Sindjar*, 202.

Êzîdî were able to organize themselves. Since then, new Êzîdî umbrella organizations have loudly raised their voices and have gotten involved in shaping the future of the region.

On February 15, 2013, the Êzîdî organized their first local councils in the Hasaka region, which is not in Afrin but in the Cizîrê. This was supported by the new Kurdish administration, and additional villages in various parts of the Cizîrê soon followed suit.[18] These associations formed the Association of the Êzîdî of West Kurdistan and Syria (Komela Êzdiyên Rojavayê Kurdistanê û Sûriye, KÊRKS), an umbrella organization close to the PKK. The Council of the Êzîdî of Syria (Encûmena Êzdiyên Sûriyê, EÊS) and the Union of the Êzîdî of Syria (Hevbendiya Êzîdiyên Suriyê, HÊS) emerged as rivals. While the HÊS has clearly had a rapprochement with both the PYD and the KÊRKS in the last two years, the EÊS still maintains its strict opposition to the PYD.

These three associations also represent very different concepts of identity. While the EÊS bases itself on traditional Êzîdî, who see the Êzîdî religion as an autonomous religious community, the KÊRKS pursues the Zoroastrian interpretation of the Êzîdî religion described above. This became clear in 2014 when the most important Êzîdî center in Afrin, the KÊRKS-affiliated Mala Êzîdîya in Afrin City, erected a life-size statue of Zoroaster in front of the building, an event that caused quite a stir, and not just among the traditional Êzîdî in Afrin but also internationally among Êzîdî organizations abroad. The HÊS is located somewhere between these two positions. Politically it is now close to the PYD, but as a splinter from the Council of the Êzîdî of Syria it still advocates a rather traditional concept of Êzîdî identity that doesn't see the Êzîdî religion as a variant of Zoroastrianism.

The Alevi

The Alevi are primarily concentrated in the small town of Mabeta and a few hamlets in the area that are all part to the subdistrict (*nāḥ iyah*) of Mabeta. At the last census, in 2004, which did not address religious affiliation, the subdistrict had more than eleven thousand inhabitants, not all of whom, however, were Alevi. The number of Alevi is probably somewhere between five thousand and ten thousand. They are genuine Alevi, a form

---

18 Sebastian Maisel, *Yezidis in Syria: Identity Building among a Double Minority* (Lanham, MD: Lexington Books, 2017), 147.

of Shiite heterodoxy that is also widespread among Turkish-, Zaza-, and Kurmancî-speaking Turkish citizens, but not among the Alawites, who are widespread in Syria or among the Arab-speaking minority of Hatay or the Çukurova in Turkey. The Alawites represent a different religious current that, beyond a loose connection with Shiite Islam, doesn't have much to do with the Anatolian Alevi or the Alevi of Mabeta.

The Alevi depart from the practice of faith of Sunni Islam and of the orthodox Twelver Shia in many ways. They don't pray in mosques but hold their religious celebrations, which they call *Cem*, in Cem houses. While the Sunni and Shia practice ritual prayer, the Alevi worship God through songs, the recitation of poems and Quranic passages, and ritual dance (*Semah*), and men and women pray and celebrate together. The Alevi regard neither the five pillars of Islam nor the sharia as binding. Compared to the Sunni and Shia mainstream, in Alevism laws and orthopraxis play a subordinate role. As a form of Islam persecuted and driven underground for centuries, Alevism must basically be seen as a popular religion that has spawned only a very few theologists and scribes. Alevi religiosity was not handed down through Quran schools and scholarly writings but through families, poems, and songs.

The center of the Alevi philosophy is the interaction between humans themselves and between humans and God, and certain pantheist ideas have also become part of Alevism. The faithful strongly recognize God in their fellow human beings.

The frequent characterization of the faith by secular Alevi intellectuals as a sort of "liberal Islam" must be qualified. Just as in Sunni and Shia Islam, there are both stricter and less strict readings and interpretations of the faith among the Alevi, but Alevi communities are generally like the others in traditionally regarding adherence to strict social rules as the educational goal. A violation of these rules can lead to the exclusion from a Cem celebration, or even from the community itself. These social rules are summarized by three commandments:

1. Control your hands: don't kill, steal, or do violence to anyone.

2. Control your tongue: don't swear, lie, or badmouth others.

3. Control your loins: faithfulness, monogamy, no extramarital sex.[19]

---

19 Thomas Schmidinger, ed., *Kurdistan im Wandel: Konflikte, Staatlichkeit, Gesellschaft und Religion zwischen Nahem Osten und Diaspora* (Vienna: Peter Lang, 2011), 54.

In matters of community organization, the Alevi are strictly divided into two groups whose membership is determined by descent. "Both practice endogamy, because their relationship is thought of as one between parents and their children. It follows that marriages between the two groups are seen as incest."[20]

In and around Mabeta, there are close to a dozen Alevi shrines whose names generally end with "Dada" (Dede): Yagmur Dada, Aslan Dada, Ali Dada, and Maryam Dada. As among the Anatolian Alevi, the clerics of the Syrian-Kurdish Alevi are also called Dede or Dada.

Even though there are no historical records about the immigration of the ancestors of the Alevi of Afrin, it seems reasonable to assume an immigration from the Alevi areas of Kurdistan, which are today part of Turkey. Some of the Alevi of Mabeta only arrived in the region in the twentieth century. In 1938, the Alevi of Mabeta took in refugees from the Dersim massacre. Eighty years later, their descendants are once again fleeing from the Turkish army.

Even after the fall of the Ottoman Empire, the Alevi of Mabeta remained in contact with the Alevi in Turkey, and religious relationships with the Anatolian Alevi were never cut off.

Just like the Êzîdî, the Alevi only began to create formal organizations in 2012. The most important of these is the Center of the Alevi of Mabeta (Navenda Elewiyan ya Navçeya Mabeta) in the small town of the same name.

Like numerous Êzîdî, many Alevi also supported the secular political system established in Afrin since 2012, with Hêvî Îbrahîm Mustefa, an Alevi from Afrin, serving as prime minister of the region.

Christians

There was a historical presence of Christians in Afrin, but it has nothing to do with the Christian community in Afrin today. Early Christian ruins testify to the fact that the region of Afrin, like the neighboring Antioch (which is now part of Turkey), is part of the core lands of early Christianity. The most important of these buildings is probably the Qal'at Sim'ān (Simon's Fortress), which is located at the border between Afrin and the areas to the south of the region held by Sunni rebel groups.

---

20 Karin Vorhoff, *Zwischen Glaube, Nation und neuer Gemeinschaft: Alevitische Identität in der Türkei der Gegenwart* (Berlin: Klaus Schwartz Verlag, 1995), 66.

This is a large Byzantine monastery, erected where, according to legend, Symeon Stylites the Elder (389–459) is believed to have lived atop a pillar for several decades. This began the trend of the "pillar saints" in Syria, which remains an allegory in contemporary usage. Even in the twentieth century, artists, including the Spanish filmmaker Luis Buñuel in his film *Simon in the Desert* (Simón del desierto), have addressed the topic.

In the Byzantine era, there was a large monastery here whose ruins are still among the most important tourist attractions in Syria. Since the beginning of the Syrian civil war, it has been at the front line between the YPG/YPJ and the Sunni rebel organizations. The shifts in control of the front line have likely led to the ruins being damaged.

In the case of today's city of Cindirês, we know of a diocese at the time of the Council of Nicaea in the year 325.

The mountains near the ancient town of Cyrrhus in the north of Afrin, where Muslims venerate the tomb of the prophet Huri, are believed to be where the monk Maron, whom both the Maronite and Roman-Catholic Churchs see as a founding father, was active. His alleged grave is near the village Beradê (Arabic: Brad) in the south of the region of Afrin, northeast of Qal'at Sim'ān. There are several church and monastery ruins in the area, among them the historically significant Great Chapel of Julianos. Until the start of the civil war, Maronite Christians from the Lebanon made the pilgrimage to the Tomb of Maron in Beradê: in 2008, on the occasion of the sixteen hundredth anniversary of the death of Saint Maron, later Lebanese president Michel Aoun was one of the prominent pilgrims. The years before the civil war even saw the construction of a small new church, and, in 2010, a statue of Saint Maron from Lebanon was placed in it. But the church only served Maronite pilgrims for a short while, since there has not been any Maronite community here for quite a while. There is no continuity between the early Christian communities of the region and later Christian communities. Under Islamic rule, the early Christians, who spoke Greek and Aramaic, either migrated to the larger urban centers or, over the years, converted to Islam. There are, however, no detailed reports about any of this.

It is well known that after the genocide against the Armenians in 1915, survivors settled in Afrin. There was an Armenian-Apostolic church and an Armenian school in the town of Afrin. But the sparse data seem to indicate that the Armenian community was never very large. In the 1958–1959 school year, only fifty students attended the school, which was run by no more than two teachers.[21]

In 1927, the Armenian liquor producer Sarkis Kiwanian began to produce Arak in Afrin, and at the start of the civil war, this most reputed Syrian anise liquor was still produced there.

In a 2015 interview with Kamal Sido of the Society for Threatened People, one of the last Armenians of Afrin shared memories of the community that existed until the 1960s and had approximately one hundred members.[22] In the second half of the 1960s, most of them emigrated to the U.S., Armenia, or Aleppo. The church fell into ruins, and the property on which it stood was sold. Finally, the ruins were removed to make way for a new building. When Kamal Sido conducted his interview with the then fifty-eight-year-old Aruth Kevork in 2015, the latter explained that his family was the last remaining Armenian family in Afrin. In 2018, the editor of the Armenian newspaper *Kantsasar*, which is published in Aleppo, Zarmig Chilaposhyan-Poghigian, claimed that there were still three Armenian families in Afrin.[23] This "increase" can possibly be explained by the flight of Armenian families from other regions in war-torn Syria. At any rate, since the late 1960s, there has been no actual Armenian community in Afrin, only individual Armenian families.

However, this does not mean that Christianity has entirely disappeared from Afrin. In 2012, with the new Evangelical Church of the Good Shepherd (Şivane Qanç), a Christian community of Kurdish converts emerged in Afrin. This community originated in Aleppo but migrated to Afrin when the war in Aleppo started. By 2018, this Kurdish Christian community had increased to a total of three hundred families. Apart from the city of Afrin, churches were also built in the small cities of Cindirês and Reco, but these communities are much smaller, and most of the Christians of the region of Afrin live in the city of Afrin. Following the Turkish invasion of the region, members of the Christian communities of Cindirês and Reco fled to the city of Afrin. It is impossible to know whether the church buildings they left behind survived the Turkish army's bombardment,

---

21 Nicola Migliorino, *(Re)Constructing Armenia in Lebanon and Syria: Ethno-Cultural Diversity and the State in the Aftermath of a Refugee Crisis* (New York: Berghahn Books, 2008), 120.
22 Schmidinger, "Militärische Expansion mit US-Unterstützung," 149.
23 "There are 3 Armenian Families in Syria's Afrin," *News*, January 25, 2018, accessed September 28, 2018, https://news.am/eng/news/432989.html.

which did severe damage, particularly in the city center of Cindirês. Most of the Christians from these two communities who had to flee found a provisional haven in the Church of Afrin, until they had to flee once more following the conquest of Afrin.

While converts face severe problems in many Islamic communities, in secular Afrin the conversion to Christianity is relatively unproblematic. The rise in conversions to Christianity since 2015 seems to have to do in part with an oppositional stance against the jihadist militias, particularly the Islamic State, but probably also represents a form of "cultural conversion." The middle and upper strata of society in particular want to "Europeanize," in an effort to stand apart from their Islamic surroundings. They frequently see Christianity as "modern" and "secular," while they regard Islam as "backward" and "fanatical." These perceptions of both the self and other seem to play an important role in the conversion to Christianity. It is interesting that these Kurds do not convert to one of the traditional Syrian churches but to an actively proselytizing Evangelical Church community under a charismatic pastor of Kurdish origin named Diyar. Pastor Diyar has raised his voice against the Turkish attacks on Afrin several times since they began and has articulated his fear that a Turkish victory could prove particularly dangerous for Christians in Afrin. "If these gangs enter Afrin, before all, they will kill Christians," a Kurdish news agency quoted him saying in early February 2018.[24]

Jewish, Alawite, and Shiite Neighbors

Unlike Cizîrê, where there was a Jewish community in Qamişlo well into the twenty-first century, and where there is still a synagogue, no Jewish community ever existed in modern Afrin. But in the Turkish town of Kilis located directly at today's national border, there was once a synagogue, and its ruins survived and served an Arabic-speaking Jewish community until the twentieth century.[25] Furthermore, the nearby metropolis of Aleppo was one of the most important centers of Jewish life in Syria. West of Afrin, in the town of Antakya (the former Antioch), which has

24 "Call from the Christians in Afrin," *AFN News*, February 2, 2018, accessed September 28, 2018, https://anfenglish.com/rojava/call-from-the-christians-in-afrin-24634.
25 Naim Güleryüz, *The Synagogues of Turkey: The Synagogues of Thrace and Anatolia* (Istanbul: Gozlem Gazetecilik Basin ve Yayin A.S., 2008), 103.

been part of Turkey since 1939, there is still a small Jewish community with an intact synagogue. At this point, the community only consists of a few more than a dozen faithful, but it is the only remaining Jewish community of the three that once surrounded the "Mountain of the Kurds." These communities, in Aleppo, Kilis, and Antakya, used Arabic as their everyday language and were oriented toward the region's urban centers. Though there might have been individual Jews who lived in between these communities temporarily, acting as business contacts between Kurds and Jews in these three urban centers, which were in turn important for the Afrin region, at least following the Islamization of the region, there has been no known settlement of Jews in the region of Afrin.

The Kurds of Afrin were also in neighborly contact with other religious communities. In Antakya and the region around it, which until 1938 was still part of the French protectorate of Syria and has been part of Turkey since 1939, there were many Arabic-speaking Alawites, members of a Shiite heterodoxy that should not be confused with the Alevi, and whose members also live in Syria, specifically, in the coastal mountains of the Ğabal al-Anṣārīya. The Syrian ruling Assad family is part of this religious minority. Under Hafiz al-Assad, the father of the current president, many Alawites gained important posts in the military, the secret services, and the police force, which has contributed to the confessionalism of the conflicts in Syria since 2001.

In the southwest, Afrin abuts the small Arabic-speaking towns of Nubl, with a population of twenty-one thousand, and az-Zahrāʾ, with thirteen thousand inhabitants, whose majority belongs to the Twelver Shia variety of Islam, the current of that religion that is the state religion in Iran and the majority religion in Iraq, Azerbaijan, and Bahrein. Because of the confessionalism of the conflict, the populations in Nubl and az-Zahrāʾ remained loyal to the regime. Both cities have been continuously held by militias loyal to Damascus, even though from 2012 to 2016 they were only an enclave within an area held by oppositional forces. For the Shiites in Nubl and az-Zahrāʾ, the Kurds in Afrin became important mediators. From July 2012 to February 2016, Afrin was the only way out for the Shiites living there. Now Nubl and az-Zahrāʾ function as the escape hatch for Kurds from Afrin who are fleeing the attacks by Turkey and its allies.

History

Early History

The oldest archaeological discoveries in the region of Afrin are to be found in the cave of Dederiyeh in the south of today's canton of Afrin, about sixty meters [196 feet] above the bottom of the Wadi Dederiyeh valley. In 1987, human and animal bones were excavated, and the human bones have been associated with at least seventeen different individuals belonging to the Neanderthal genus. In August 1993, an archaeological research group under the direction of Takeru Akazawa discovered the almost complete skeleton of a child that was more than fifty thousand years old. Like this first one, a second child skeleton found in 1997–1998 showed signs of ritual burial.[1]

The Dederiyeh findings not only belong to the oldest human findings in the Middle East but also to the first indications that fifty thousand years ago the Neanderthals were carrying out ritual burials and possibly even had a spiritual conception of an afterlife. However, most of the bone findings were remnants from hunting quarry. They could be assigned to wild sheep and goats, gazelles, wild boars, deer, and aurochs, each appearing in different layers and thus giving the archaeologists important information about the diet and hunting habits of the earlier inhabitants of the region. They also provide information about climatic changes: apparently, dry

---

1   Osamu Kondo and Hajime nishida, "Ontogenetic Variation in the Dederiyeh Neandertal Infants: Postcranial Evidence," in *Patterns of Growth and Development in the Genus Homo*, ed. Jennifer L. Thompson, Gail E. Krovitz, and Andrew J. Nelson (Cambridge: Cambridge University Press, 2003), 386–411.

steppe phases are followed by moister periods, with forests and forest dwellers, including wild boars and aurochs, being hunted.

The Neanderthal findings in the cave at the Wadi Dederiyeh are, along with the findings in the cave of Shanidar in Iraqi Kurdistan, the findings in Ksar Akil in Lebanon, the Behistun cave in Iran, and several findings in Israel, the only findings of Neanderthals in the Middle East and are thus among the oldest archaeological sites in the region testifying to human settlement.

The hills of Afrin belong to the region that that the U.S. archaeologist James Henry Breasted described as the "fertile crescent" at the beginning of the twentieth century. He was referring to the area north of the Syrian desert, in which, thanks to the winter rain, the Neolithic Revolution took place from the twelfth millennium BC on, turning hunter-gathers into tillers of the soil and breeders of cattle. Here people domesticated goats, sheep, and then cattle and pigs and began to cultivate barley, single-grain wheat, and emmer. And it was here that the first permanent human settlements and cities emerged.

Hurrians, Hittites, and Assyrians

Since around 3400 BC, at least the west of the Kurd Dagh region has been part of the sphere of influence of Alalakh, a Bronze Age city on the plain of Amuq in the Antakya/Hatay region, where the trade routes to Anatolia from Aleppo, Mesopotamia, and Palestine converged, and which today is part of Turkey. Even though the political history of this kingdom can as of yet be reconstructed only with difficulty because of the lack of sources, we can assume that the region of the Kurd Dagh was part of the narrower sphere of influence of this trading state.

The Hurrians were present in northern Mesopotamia by the end of the third millennium BC and started to expand to the west in 1800 BC, reaching the north of Syria and advancing into Israel in the process. In the fifteenth century BC, today's region of Afrin fell under the influence of the Mittani Empire in the north of Mesopotamia, which ruled over a mixed population of Hurrians, Assyrians, Hittites, and Amorites until the mid-fourteenth century BC. Under the Great King Šuppiluliuma I, northwestern Syria was finally integrated into the Hittite Empire. The most important Hittite archaeological site in Afrin is Tal Ain Dara, where there have been findings dating back to the thirteenth century BC. Even after the Hittites, the city continued to play a key role, and it contains, among other things, a temple of the Mesopotamian goddess Ištar, who was venerated as the goddess of war and sexuality. Findings at this site date back to the Hellenistic time. On January 26, 2018, Tal Ain Dara, one of the archaeological sites with more than just regional importance, was attacked by the Turkish Air Force. According to the Syrian Observatory for Human Rights, 60 percent of the excavations were destroyed.[2] The Turkish military at first denied these accusations and claimed that it never attacked historical sites or buildings. But BBC film recordings made using a drone confirm the far-reaching destruction of the historical temple site.

For many Kurds from Afrin, the early settlement of the region from the north is of great significance for their national identity and represents an opportunity to dissociate themselves from the Arabs from the south. Even though there are no unequivocal indications of a historical continuity between the Anatolian population groups and today's Kurds, in the twentieth century and in a region with increasingly ethnic and confessional conflict the reference to historical empires and population groups has become increasingly important. Different from many other Kurds who, citing the Russian Orientalist Vladimir Fedorovich Minorsky, trace their origins back to the Medes, among the Kurds in Afrin there is a tendency to refer back to the Hurrians, whose language is different from Kurdish and is not Indo-European but also does not belong to the Semitic language family shared by Assyrians and Arabs.

East of the Kurdish region of Afrin, near Tal Rifaat, in an area conquered by the SDF in 2016, is the site of what was probably once the most important town in Arpad, one of the central cities of the ninth century BC Aramaic Empire, Bit Agusi, a town that is also mentioned in three books of the Hebrew Bible.[3] Even though the connection of Arpad to Tal Rifaat is not confirmed with any certainty, it is reasonably clear that Afrin was also a part of this small Aramaic state. Between the ninth and the seventh centuries BC, the region was part of the Neo-Assyrian Empire, and after the latter's destruction by the Medes and Babylonians, Syria was absorbed into the Neo-Babylonian Empire, which was finally conquered by the Persian Achaemenid Empire in 539 BC.

---

2   "Syria War: Turkish Air Strikes 'Damage Ancient Afrin Temple,'" *BBC News*, January 29, 2018, accessed September 28, 2018, https://www.bbc.com/news/world-middle-east-42858265.

3   Kings 2, 18:34 and 19:13; Isaiah 10:9, 36:19, and 37:13; Jeremiah 49:23.

Hellenism and Roman Empire

The conquest of the Achaemenid Empire by Alexander the Great, who was able to take over today's Syria following the battle of Issus in the years 332 and 331 BC, was the beginning of the integration of Syria into the Hellenistic world. Under the rule of Alexander's successors, the Seleucids, cultural influences from the Greek and Persian sphere mixed with the influence of the Aramaic-language populations of the Middle East, laying the foundation for a cultural development that continued under Roman rule. Some authors, such as the Syrian Kurdologist Ismet Chérif Vanly, place the immigration of Kurdish tribes into the Kurd Dagh region at this early date, tying it to the mercenaries employed by the Seleucids.[4]

Finally, the slow decline of the Seleucids in the second century BC led to the occupation of the region by the Armenian king Tigranes II (Tigranes the Great) in 83 BC, but he was expelled by the Romans in 69 BC. The Romans once again installed a Seleucid ruler as their vassal, before declaring Syria a Roman province in 63 BC. The seat of the procurator of the Roman province of Syria was the city of Antioch, which became one of the most important towns of the East Roman Empire and was located only twenty-five kilometers [fifteen miles] from the Kurd Dagh, where olives were already being grown at that time.

With the partition of the province of Syria, the hilly land of Afrin became part of the province Syria Phoenice. It continued to be the hinterland of the capital Antioch, which at the time was, along with Alexandria and Constantinople, the most important city of the eastern Mediterranean area. But the region around Antioch also became one of the earliest centers of Christianity in the Roman Empire. It is said that the first Christian community around Paul, Barnabas, and Petrus gathered in the Grotto of St. Peter in the northeast of Antioch, which has survived as a cave church until today. According to the Acts of the Apostles, Antioch was the place where non-Jews converted to Christianity for the first time,[5] as well as where the followers of Jesus began to call themselves "Christians" (Greek: Christianoi) for the first time.[6]

---

4   Ismet Chérif Vanly, "The Kurds in Syria and Lebanon," in *The Kurds: A Contemporary Overview*, ed. Philip Kreyenbroek (London: Routledge, 1992), 116.
5   Apostles 11: 20–25.
6   Apostles 11: 26.

Christian and Islamic Rule

It was not just Antioch that belonged to the earliest Christian centers, the same was also true of its general surroundings. Thus, the hilly lands of the Kurd Dagh were already a key Christian refuge in the first centuries AD.

The region of Afrin is home to several archaeologically valuable early Christian ruins, among them the city of Cyrrhus, north of Afrin, the ruins of the monastery of St. Simon, and another site near Beradê in the south. As a part of the region that predominantly hosted Christian churches that were regarded as heretical and were in part persecuted by the imperial church after the ecclesiastical schisms at the Councils of Ephesus and Chalcedon, in 431 and 451, respectively, it was relatively easy for seventh-century Muslims to integrate the population—which nonetheless remained predominantly Christian for quite some time—into the Islamic Empire after the conquest of Syria under the caliphs Abu Bakr and Umar.

Under the rule of Caliph Umar, the region of Afrin was annexed to the Islamic Empire in 637. That was the year that a cavalry under the prophet's companion Abū 'Ubayda 'Āmir b. 'Abd Allāh b. al-Jarrāh of the Quraishiti clan of the Banū l-Hārith conquered the villages on the Cûmê plane, after which the town of Cyrrhus submitted to the Muslims without resistance following an agreement between the military leader and a priest in Cyrrhus.[7]

In the late eleventh century, today's region of Afrin became part of the Antioch princedom created by the crusaders. The European crusaders used the former St. Simon monastery in the south of the region as a crusader castle for their—ultimately unsuccessful—attacks on Aleppo. However, more than a hundred years before the end of the princedom of Antioch in 1268, the region of Afrin had already been conquered by the Turkmen dynasty of the Zengids, under the leadership of 'Imād ad-Dīn Zangī, who succeeded in seizing large swathes of Mesopotamia and Aleppo after the fall of Mosul in 1128.[8]

After the victory of Saladin, a Kurdish prince from what is now central Iraq, over the Zengids near the Horns of Hama in April 1175 and

---

7   Muhammed Abdo Ali, *Jabal al-Ākrād (Afrīn): Dirasat tārihiyah ijtimāiyah taw-thiqiyah* (Suleymania, IQ: 2009), 51.

8   P.M. Holt, *The Age of the Crusades: The Near East from the Eleventh Century to 1517* (London: Routledge, 2013), 40.

his conquest of A'zaz in June 1176, the Kurd Dagh region fell under his influence. In 1187, he would finally liberate Jerusalem, after which he founded the dynasty of the Ayyubids, which remained in power until the mid-thirteenth century. It was, however, only in May 1182 that Saladin was able to conquer Aleppo after a short siege, thus securing his power in the north of Syria, including the region of Afrin.

Rule of the Mendî under the Ayyubids and Mamluks

Given the lack of written sources, it is impossible to know with any certainty when Kurds started to settle Afrin. It is, however, clear that many Kurdish warriors came to Syria in the wake of Saladin, leading to the emergence of entire Kurdish neighborhoods in Aleppo and Damascus. It makes sense to also see the settlement of the Kurd Dagh by Kurdish tribes in this light, particularly because the retreat of the crusaders led to the emigration of a part of the Christian population in the region, and because the region had been very thinly settled under the rule of the crusaders. While some authors date the Kurdish immigration into the region as early as the time of the Seleucids in the second and third centuries BC,[9] the defeat of the crusaders and the establishment of the rule of Saladin is probably the latest possible point for the Kurdish immigration into today's region of Afrin. It would also be a fair assumption that the partially depopulated former border regions that had been characterized for decades by the shifting front line separating crusaders and Muslims were again settled by Kurdish followers of Saladin, or that there was at least an additional influx. At any rate, by the late Middle Ages at the latest the hill land of Afrin was almost certainly characterized by a pronounced presence of the Kurds.

Under the Ayyubids, the Kurd Dagh region formed part of the princedom of the Mendî, which is also called the princedom of Kilis and A'zaz.[10] In the *Sharafnāma*, a chronicle of princes created by the Kurdish poet and historian Sharaf ud-Dīn Khān al-Bitlīsī in 1597, the claim is made that the dynasty of the Mendî was founded by two brothers, Şemsedîn and Behdîn, who had supposedly come to the region from Colemêrg (Turkish: Hakkari). The center of this Kurdish dynasty was the border town Kilis, which is now located in Turkey. But apart from today's Afrin, the dynasty

---

9   Vanly, "The Kurds in Syria and Lebanon," 116.
10 Ali, *Jabal al-Ākrād*, 56.

also ruled over the linguistically mixed regions further to the east around A'zaz, where there are Arab, Kurdish, and Turkmen villages to this very day. The Kurdish Mendî ruled over a religiously and linguistically diverse population that consisted of Muslims, Christians, Êzîdî, Alevi, and Jews who spoke Arabic, Kurdish, Armenian, and Turkish. At least parts of the tribe of the Mendî were Êzîdî.

This dynasty even outlasted the Mongol invasions. Thirteenth- and fourteenth-century records indicate that there were repeated conflicts between the region's Muslim Mendî and the Êzîdî. Finally, the local Êzîdî sheikhs allied themselves with the Burji Mamluks then ruling in Egypt, a Circassian Mamluk dynasty that had taken power in Cairo in 1382. But the Mendî were still able to carry on as the local rulers in the region.

Even though Qasim Beğ, who at the time of Selim I was the local ruler of the Mendî and was thus also in control of the Kurd Dagh, allied himself with the rapidly expanding Ottoman rule, he was soon murdered on the orders of Selim.[11] His successor, Canpolat Beğ, who ruled from 1516 to his death in 1572, and whose rule is testified to by a mosque and Sufi-Tekke in Kilis, which was built by and named after him and exists to this day,[12] was able to safeguard the rule of his family in the Ottoman controlled region, ensuring that the Mendî remained the local rulers and the leading political force in the region, even under Ottoman rule.

Afrin in the Ottoman Empire

Beginning in 1516, after the defeat of the Burji Mamluks at the hands of the Ottomans, Syria became part of the Ottoman Empire. But here, at the fringes of the Empire, there was no uniform penetration of the territory by the new rulers. The Empire was primarily present in the towns and along the most important traffic routes, while peripheral areas increasingly assumed an independent existence under local rulers. Thus, in the sixteenth century, Druze emirs in today's Lebanon acted in an increasingly autonomous fashion, with many of the areas settled by Kurds being autonomous princedoms or tribal areas only loosely connected to the center of the empire. In the Kurd Dagh region, the Mendî remained in power as Kurdish local princes under Ottoman suzerainty. Canpolat Beğ

---

11   Ali, *Jabal al-Ākrād*, 60.
12   T.A. Sinclair, *Eastern Turkey: An Architectural and Archaeological Survey*, vol. 6 (London: Pindar Press, 1990), 114.

secured the influence of his dynasty until his death in 1572. In 1603, his successor Hussein defended Kilis and Aleppo against an uprising of the Janissaries, the elite Ottoman troops, and was rewarded for this with the office of Governor of Aleppo, although he would be executed shortly thereafter, in 1605.[13] In response to this, there was an uprising led by his nephew Ali Canpolat, who is often called Canpolatoğlu (son of Canpolat) in Turkish sources, who tried to establish independent rule in the region around Aleppo and Kilis, as well as in the Kurd Dagh. He managed to capture Aleppo but was ultimately defeated in 1607 and executed in 1611.[14] With Ali Canpolat, the last local ruler of Kilis from the Mendî dynasty died.

His descendants emigrated to today's Lebanon and became an important noble family among the local Druze. The Jumblatts, who gave birth to the two most important Lebanese Druze politicians of the twentieth century, Kamal and Walid Jumblatt, are descendants of Canpolat Beğ. The family's Kurdish descent is still known today both by Kurds and in Lebanon itself.

After the end of Mendî rule, their territory was integrated into the Eyâlet Aleppo, which had been in existence since 1534. With this, today's region of Afrin came under the direct administration of an Ottoman province. In 1620, a Kurd from the Rubari lineage of the tribe of the Barwari was appointed as the local ruler of Kilis. After his dismissal or death, his descendants settled down in a castle in Basûtê, twelve kilometers [seven and a half miles] to the south of today's city of Afrin, and ruled the Afrin River valley, with its fertile plain.[15]

In 1736, the clan of the Genc displaced the Rubari from Basûtê and established their rule over the Afrin valley, the heart of the region. In 1742, the family of Haj Omar from the tribe of the Raşwan assumed control over the Afrin valley, and eventually over Kilis until the Ottomans reintegrated the region into their own administrative system in a more direct fashion in 1866, incorporating it into the Vilâyet Aleppo, which had been founded in 1864 during the Tanzimat Reforms. Within the Vilâyet, Afrin

---

13 Bruce Masters, "Semi-Autonomous Forces in the Arab Provinces," in *The Cambridge History of Turkey, vol. 3: The Late Ottoman Empire 1603–1839*, ed. Suraiya N. Faroqhi (Cambridge: Cambridge University Press, 2006), 191.

14 Ali, *Jabal al-Ākrād*, 64.

15 Ali, *Jabal al-Ākrād*, 65.

formed a part of the Kaza of Kilis,[16] which in turn was part of the Sanjak of Aleppo.

During this phase, as a new social order was established in the Kurd Dagh region, the importance of the Kurdish tribes steadily declined. Local feudal lords replaced the tribes as the most important economic and political actors. Then under the new land law of 1858, which was enacted as part of the Tanzimat Reforms to regulate the private registration of land in the Ottoman Empire, individual men registered large estates in their names. Throughout the Ottoman Empire, villages and estates that had hitherto been regarded as collective property were registered by local notables as their private property. Small peasants who could not read or write either did not have their land registered or were simply taken advantage of by the ağas and urban merchants.[17] In the case of Afrin, this meant that the Kurdish tribes, with their relatively egalitarian organization, whose ağas also had to take into account the common good of their respective tribes, ceased to be the central organizational form of Kurdish society and were replaced by individual large landowners, some of them coming from the families of the old ağas, who were legitimized by the state, and on whom the landless peasants were dependent. Feudalism in Afrin was a relatively new development at the time and can be regarded as a direct consequence of the land law of 1858. The new feudal families of the Şiekk, Ismail, Saaydo, Mimi, Ammo, Rubari, and Kanj that emerged from this shift in the economic and social situation would constitute the Kurdish upper class in Afrin until the era of the French protectorate.[18]

The beginning of the twentieth century saw the first stirring of nationalism among Kurdish intellectuals and tribal leaders. Partially inspired by other nationalisms in the Ottoman Empire, this first generation of Kurdish nationalism was still much more tribal than national. The foundation of the Hamidiye regiments in 1890 provided these Kurdish

---

16 Kaza (Arabic: *qaḍā*) could be translated as "district." The kaza formed a subordinate administrative unit of the Ottoman Empire. Normally, several kazas taken together form a *sanjak*, a unit that was in turn subordinated to a *vilâyet*. In the Turkish Republic, the notion of "kaza" was replaced by "*ilçe*" in the 1920s. Today Kilis is a border town in Turkey, in the northeast of Afrin.

17 Peter Krois, *Kultur und literarische Übersetzung—eine Wechselbeziehung: Österreichische und syrisch-arabische Kontextualisierung von Kurzgeschichten Zakariyyā Tāmirs* (Berlin: Lit Verlag, 2012), 77.

18 Ali, *Jabal al-Ākrād*, 70.

tribal leaders with their own armed troops, even though these were meant to be the sultan's auxiliary troops and functioned as such, for example, against the Armenians from 1894 to 1896. For the Kurds in Aleppo, Afrin, and the Kurdish settlements around Aleppo, İbrahim Paşa Mîllî played an important role in these developments. Although his tribe, the Mîllî, were centered further to the east, it has been suggested that he harbored aspirations to create a Kurdish state around the region of Aleppo, although, if true, nothing concrete ever came of it.[19]

Afrin under the French Protectorate

At the end of World War I, Syria was initially occupied by British troops and their Arab allies. Afrin was taken over by the Indian Division but by 1919 had been handed over to French troops stationed in the village of Qitmê. Some Kurds from the region joined Mustafa Kemal's Kuvâyı Milliye to fight the French garrisoned there, with armed confrontations between Kurds and the French taking place near the villages Gelî Tîra and Hesarê. In the end, however, the attempts to integrate Afrin into the Turkish civil war were unsuccessful, because the French managed to establish good relations with some of the Kurdish ağas and set up their own district with the support local Kurdish militias.[20]

In 1920, Syria was declared a French mandate area at the San Remo conference, and this was eventually confirmed by the League of Nations in 1922. Parallel to this, King Feisal I from the onetime Moroccan Hashemite dynasty tried to establish the Arab Kingdom of Syria in today's Syria, Lebanon, Palestine, and Jordan but was defeated by the French troops in the battle of Maysalun (twenty-five kilometers [fifteen and a half miles] west of Damascus) on July 24, 1920. Afrin, which the Arab Kingdom of Syria continued to see as part of the Vilâyet Aleppo, thus came under French rule.

The French at first assigned Afrin to the State of Aleppo (État d'Alep) founded in the north of today's Syria in 1920. The French imposed as ruler the seventy-five-year-old Kamil Pasha al-Qudsi, who came from a traditional religious family of feudal lords in Aleppo, and who as a former officer of the Ottoman army and the local boss of Sultan Abdülhamid's

---

19   Philip Mansel, *Aleppo: The Rise and Fall of Syria's Great Merchant City* (London: I.B. Tuarus & Co., 2016), 44f.

20   Ali, *Jabal al-Ākrād*, 76.

secret service had been active against the Hashemites.[21] In reality, he and his two successors, Mustafa Bey Barmada and Mar'i Pascha al-Malla, were subservient to a French delegate who had a say on all important political decisions. After an uprising led by the Arab nationalist Ibrāhīm Hanānū from Aleppo, the State of Aleppo was integrated into the Syrian Federation (Fédération syrienne), which also included the State of Damascus and the State of the Alawites (État des Alaouites) on the Syrian coast, which on December 1, 1924, became the State of Syria, but nonetheless, continued to be subjected to the French protectorate.

Afrin's border with Turkey was only fixed with the Treaty of Lausanne in 1923. This border cut through a territory that had been unified since before the Ottoman era. It separated Kurdish tribal areas from each other and cut the Syrian Kurd Dagh off from its administrative center of Kilis. This border would be traversed by smugglers for decades and continued to be challenged by the local population until Syria achieved independence. The back-and-forth border traffic between the villages in the Syrian part of the Kurd Dagh and the neighboring Kurdish villages in the Turkish province Gaziantep, as well as in Hatay (which was handed over to Turkey in 1938–1939), was uncontrolled for many years.[22]

The new borders transferred the town of Kilis to Turkey, costing the region its traditional center. Therefore, the administration was at first moved to Qitmê, and then via Meydana, Mabata, Gewrika, and Maratê to today's town of Afrin.[23] The new town gained its name (the bridged one) from its Roman Kopriyê bridge. The official buildings for the new district administration were completed between 1925 and 1927.

The decision of the French authorities to establish a new small-town center for the region of Afrin also made it attractive to refugees stranded in the area. Survivors of the genocide carried out by the government of the Young Turks of the Ottoman Empire in 1915 were the city's first new inhabitants,[24] simultaneously making it the historical base of

---

21 Philip Shukri Khouri, *Syria and the French Mandate: The Politics of Arab Nationalism, 1920–1945* (Princeton, NJ: Princeton University Press, 1987), 99.

22 Katharina Lange, "Peripheral Experiences: Everyday Life in Kurd Dagh (Northern Syria) during the Allied Occupation in the Second World War," in *The World in World Wars: Perspectives, Experiences and Perceptions from Asia and Africa*, ed. Heike Liebau (Leiden, NL: Brill, 2010), 404.

23 Ali, *Jabal al-Ākrād*, 113.

24 Ali, *Jabal al-Ākrād*, 117.

the Armenian-Apostolic community that would last until the 1960s. In addition to these Armenian refugees, during the 1920s additional Kurdish refugees who had been expelled from Turkey during the Kurdish uprisings moved to the region. As a result, the small market town became the new economic and political center of the region.

The creation of the State of Syria in 1924 was the beginning of the end of the original French protectorate policy that had initially worked toward decentralization. With a new constitution, the State of Syria became the Republic of Syria in 1930, and its first parliament included three Kurdish deputies from the early Kurdish nationalist organization Xoybûn. This organization, which was founded in 1927 in today's Lebanon, and which, not least in the form of Armenian Dashnaks,[25] was primarily supported by exiles from Turkey, sought to create a Kurdish state. It must be seen as the first modern Kurdish nationalist organization active in both Syria and Turkey. Because of the organization's anti-Turkish orientation, the French mandate tolerated Xoybûn despite its nationalist goals.[26] Hassan Aouni from the Kurd Dagh was elected to the Syrian parliament,[27] integrating the region of Afrin into Kurdish politics right from the outset as a supporter of the demand of Kurds in Syria for autonomy or independence. During the time of the mandate, however, initiatives for autonomy for Syrian Kurds were only a sideshow to the major political conflict around Syrian independence from France. Any Kurdish political movement inevitably had to enunciate a position on that question.

In the 1930s, the Muridin (Kurdish: Murûdan) movement against the French led by Ali Ghalib, which was supported by Turkey and developed contacts with Ibrāhīm Hanānū's anticolonial National Bloc (Arabic:

---

25 Members of the Armenian Revolutionary Federation (Heghapoch-agan Daschnakzutjun), a left nationalist party founded in 1890 that was to become the most important Armenian party in the Ottoman Empire at the beginning of the twentieth century. Beginning in 1894, it carried out armed actions in support of an autonomous Armenian state. Originally, it cooperated with the Young Turks but would ultimately organized a large part of the armed resistance against the 1915 genocide.

26 Özlem Belçim Galip, *Imagining Kurdistan: Identity, Culture and Society* (London: I.B. Taurus & Co., 2015), 56.

27 Vahe Tachjian, *Le France en Cilicie et en Haute-Mésopotamie: Aux confins de la Turquie, de la Syrie et de l'Iraq (1919–1933)* (Paris: Éditions Karthala, 2004), 394.

al-kutla al-wataniyya), played an important role in Afrin.[28] How the Kurds in Afrin evaluate its role today varies. While some hold the Muridin movement in esteem as a national movement, the supporters of the PYD tend to regard it as a Turkish proxy that they suspect primarily pursued Turkish interests. The armed activities of this group were related to Turkish plans to separate the Kurd Dagh and the Sanjak of Alexandrette (Antakya and Iskenderun) from Syria and to annex it to the Turkish Republic. Finally, after the French had handed over the Sanjak of Alexandrette to Turkey via its transitional status of the Republic of Hatay in 1938–1939, the group lost Turkey's support and the movement dwindled. That said, the Muridin movement should probably not be understood simply as an instrument of Turkey, as it actually did have a basis in some sections of the Kurdish population of Afrin.

In 1941, Syria became a theatre of World War II for five short weeks. After the capitulation of France and the armistice on July 22, 1940, Syria initially remained under the control of the French collaborator regime in Vichy. The British-led offensive on Syria under the command of Henry Maitland Wilson began on June 8, 1941 and ended in victory five weeks and approximately 2,000 deaths later. By mid-July, Syria—and therefore, Afrin—was under Allied occupation. As a result, the border near Afrin, which was difficult to monitor turned into an escape route from Syria into Turkey for fighters loyal to the Axis. The Kurd Dagh region regularly saw the arrest of deserters from Turkey who fled to Syria and of Syrian deserters attempting to escape to Turkey.[29] To enforce better border control, the local population was registered. Thus, businesspeople in Afrin and villagers and peasants who came to the market were forced to carry identity cards or risk arrest.[30]

These increased controls provoked protests from some local people. Thus, on April 14, 1944, a major police raid sparked a demonstration in the Afrin market to protest police abuse of the population.[31] Conflicts between Allied soldiers and the local population also erupted when soldiers were drunk. For example, on Christmas 1941, inebriated Australian soldiers

---

28 Roger Lescot, "Le Kurd Dagh et le Mouvement Mouroud," *Studio Kurdica* (1988): 101–25.
29 Lange, "Peripheral Experiences: Everyday Life in Kurd Dagh," 407.
30 Ibid.
31 Ibid., 408.

stationed in Afrin and A'zaz rioted, badgered the population, and robbed stores in the two cities.[32]

Even though the July 25, 1941, De Gaulle-Lyttelton agreement had de facto handed the military command of the Allied Forces in the Levant over to the British,[33] locally the rivalry between the British and the French military continued until the end of the war. Politically, however, the region remained largely quiet throughout this period.

After the end of the war, many of the Muridin returned from Turkey to Afrin and participated in the construction of a new Syria. Even though De Gaulle had promised Syria its independence, after the conquest of the country by British troops, the French protectorate had at first been reestablished. It was only in 1946, once the war had ended, that Syria was granted its independence.

Afrin as Part of Independent Syria

Syria received its independence as a parliamentary democracy. Various shades of Arab nationalism played an important political role, but initially they did not entirely dominate the political arena of the country. For example, the Communist Party was attractive to young Kurds. However, on April 11, 1949, this parliamentary democracy was aborted for the first time by a military coup led by Husnī az-Za'īm, who, with the support of the CIA, sent President Shukrī al-Quwatlī into exile.

In 1957, with the Democratic Party of the Kurds in Syria (Kurdish: Partîya Dêmokrat a Kurd li Sûriyê, PDKS), the first explicitly Kurdish party was founded in the Cizîrê.[34] It was, however, never formally recognized and was not allowed to participate in elections. The parties that were to emerge from diverse splinters of this party always had their center of gravity in the east of the Kurdish territories in Syria. From a geographical point of view, the Cizîrê was much closer to the Kurdish areas of Iraq and Iran than the other Syrian Kurdish areas, a fact that fostered a greater affinity with the political movements and parties in those areas. Afrin, on the other hand, was and continued to be politically focused on the adjacent

---

32 *Bulletin Hebdomadaire d'Information*, Alep, no. 21, December 27, 1941.
33 Robin Bidwell, *Dictionary of Modern Arab History: An A to Z of over 2,000 Entries from 1798 to the Present Day* (London: Routledge, 2010), 124.
34 Thomas Schmidinger, ed., *Kurdistan im Wandel: Konflikte, Staatlichkeit, Gesellschaft und Religion zwischen Nahem Osten und Diaspora* (Vienna: Peter Lang, 2011), 68.

Kurdish areas in Turkey. Unlike in the Cizîrê, in Afrin the sister parties of the Iraqi Kurdish parties were never able to establish a mass base.

At any rate, none of these parties were able to play a role in all of Syria. The old elites were essentially challenged by the Arab nationalist parties, such as the Arab Socialist Ba'ath Party (Arabic: al-hizb al-ba'th al-'arabī al-ishtirākī), the Syrian Social-Nationalist Party (Arabic: al-hizb as-Sūrī al-Qaumī al-Iǧtimā'ī), and the Communist Party (Arabic: al-hizb aš-šuyū'ī as-sūrī). Initially, the communists, under the leadership of the Kurd Khalid Bakdash from Damascus, were also an attractive alternative to Arab nationalism for young Kurds in Afrin.

In 1958, the Arab nationalists finally pushed through the unification of Syria with Gamāl'Abd an-Nāsir's Egypt, constituting the United Arab Republic (UAR), which, however, existed only until September 1961, before falling to yet another coup. The radical Arab nationalists lost the first free elections after independence was regained in December 1961. Syria had felt cheated by Egypt in the UAR, and for a time let go of the dream of Arab unity. The two victors were the old established parties, namely, the very ideologically diverse but predominantly liberal People's Party (Hizb ash-sha'b), which won in thirty-three mandates, and the conservative Syrian National Party (Hizb al-watanī), which took twenty-one mandates. With ten mandates, the Islamic Muslim Brotherhood scored an unexpected success. Because no explicitly Kurdish party had run, all the mandates in the province al-Hasaka—and thus also in the Cizîrê—went to independent candidates of differing ethnic origins. The two mandates in the district 'Ayn al-'arab (Kurdish: Kobanê) also went to independent candidates, while the three mandates of the district of Afrin were won by three Kurdish candidates from the People's Party. The victor in Jarābulus, a mixed district, with Arab, Kurdish, and Turkish populations, was also an independent candidate.[35] Among other things, the electoral results show the relative weakness of the PDKS in Afrin. While independent candidates close to this party were elected in the Cizîrê, the Kurdish candidates in Afrin were part of the ruling Arab People's Party, which represented the old elites of the country.

After these elections, Arab nationalism began to recover. The Ba'ath Party in particular managed to assert itself as a rival to the Nasserists and

---

35 Yitzkhak Oron, ed., *Middle East Record 1961*, vol. 2 (Jerusalem: Israel Program for Scientific Translations, 1961), 503ff.

to gain more and more ground. Even before the party's coup in March 1963, Arab nationalists had again gained influence in the government and the military. Afrin, however, was not as much a target of the Arab nationalists' anti-Kurdish measures as the Cizîrê, on which they focused. In Afrin, the Arabization policy of the Syrian government was less consistently applied than in the Kurdish areas further to the east. Since Afrin was an area far removed from these regions, and the Kurds in Afrin had very limited connections to the Kurdish movements in Iraq, the Kurdish presence in Afrin was apparently perceived as less of a threat than that in the Cizîrê.

The special 1962 census, which cost 120 thousand Kurds their Syrian citizenship,[36] was carried out exclusively in the Cizîrê. The Kurds in Afrin were thus not confronted with the pursuant problem of statelessness. While in the Cizîrê, beginning in 1965, the expulsion of Kurds and the settlement of loyal Arabs established an "Arab Belt" at the border with Turkey and Iraq,[37] in Afrin there were no such resettlements. This is one of the reasons why Afrin remained largely inhabited by Kurds until 2018. Arab war refugees from other parts of Syria only began to settle in the area in 2012.

Something else that incited many Kurdish notables against the regime was land expropriations. These hit many Kurdish landowners, who lost the land that their ancestors had appropriated in the second half of the nineteenth century as a consequence of the land law of 1858. Unlike other Kurdish areas of Syria, however, in Afrin this land was not handed over to Arab settlers but was primarily given to local Kurdish small farmers.[38]

All of this doesn't mean, however, that the Arab nationalism of the Ba'ath Party had passed Afrin by without a trace. In Afrin, as elsewhere, education was exclusively in Arabic, and Kurdish was marginalized from the public sphere. In 1977, the Syrian Ministry of the Interior decreed the Arabization of non-Arabic names in Afrin in its Directive no. 15801.[39] From that point until the retreat of the Syrian troops in 2012, all Kurdish villages and cities had official Arab names.

---

36 Thomas Schmidinger, *Krieg und Revolution in Syrisch-Kurdistan: Analysen und Stimmen aus Rojava* (Vienna: Mandelbaum Verlag, 2014), 79.

37 Ibid., 83.

38 Harriet Allsopp, *The Kurds of Syria: Political Parties and Identities in the Middle East* (London: I.B. Tauris, 2014): 26.

39 Kerim Yildiz, *The Kurds in Syria: The Forgotten People* (London: Pluto Press, 2005), 117.

The PKK in Afrin

While in the Cizîrê in particular, the regime tried to keep the Kurdish parties that were active in the underground under control, in Afrin the political development in the neighboring state of Turkey once more played a decisive role. On November 27, 1978, Abdullah Öcalan, Cemil Bayık, Mehmet Karasungur, Selim Çürükkaya, Şahin Dönmez, Mehmet Hayri Durmuş, Baki Karer, Şahin Durmuş, Sakine Cansız, and sixteen other activists founded the Workers' Party of Kurdistan (Kurdish: Partiya Karkerên Kurdistanê, PKK), which intended to fight for the national liberation of Kurdistan on the basis of a Marxist-Leninist program. In July 1979, after the arrest of Şahin Dönmez and before the military coup of 1980, Abdullah Öcalan fled to Syria.[40]

He was followed by a number of Kurdish activists, whose ranks were further swelled by additional oppositionists after the Turkish military coup on September 12, 1980. Öcalan managed to gain the support of the Syrian regime, assuring the latter that he would concentrate on the struggle against Turkey and refrain from interfering in internal Syrian matters. The Syrian regime under Hafiz al-Assad regarded Öcalan and the PKK primarily as a bargaining chip in its struggle with Turkey, by whose Southeastern Anatolian Project (Güneydoğu Anadolu Projesi, GAP) it felt threatened. Upon completion, this regional development project in the Kurdish areas of southeast Anatolia, which has been on the drawing board since the end of the 1970s, and which was launched at the beginning of the 1980s, will include twenty-two dams and nineteen hydroelectric plants on the Euphrates and the Tigris, rivers that flow to Syria and Iraq. This project will give Turkey control over the most important water reserves of the Middle East.[41]

In order to increase the pressure on Turkey, the Syrian regime began to support the PKK. The PKK was given the opportunity to have its cadre in Lebanon trained by the Popular Front for the Liberation of Palestine (PFLP).[42] After the closing of the so-called Mahsum-Korkmaz Academy in the Lebanese Beqaa Valley at the beginning of the 1990s, Öcalan, who, as noted above, fled to Syria in 1979, had, in fact, spent most of his time

---

40 Aliza Marcus, *Blood and Belief: The PKK and the Kurdish Fight for Independence* (New York: New York University Press, 2007), 48.
41 Schmidinger, *Krieg und Revolution in Syrisch-Kurdistan*, 91.
42 Ibid., 92.

since then in Lebanon, had his headquarters in Damascus and directed all party activity from there. The Syrian regime, for its part, not only supported the PKK but also other opponents of Turkey, such as the Armenian Secret Army for the Liberation of Armenia (ASALA), with which the PKK cooperated in the 1980s. While many leftist Turkish exiles did not woo the support of Damascus for fear of becoming instruments of the Syrian regime,[43] Öcalan built his guerilla army with the Syrian support and brought this army back to Turkey via Iraq in 1984.

Within Syria, the regime largely gave the PKK a free hand as long as the group remained loyal and directed its political and military actions against Turkey. Apparently, the regime in Damascus saw this as a way to divert political attention onto its Turkish rival, while at the same time weakening the Kurdish parties in Syria.

In the process, the PKK primarily succeeded establishing bases in those regions that, into the 1980s, had been neglected by the various Kurdish parties in Syria that over the years had splintered from the historical Democratic Party of the Kurds in Syria (PDKS). The fragmented Kurdish parties of the 1980s—a party with the same name as the PDKS, the Democratic Party of the Kurds in Syria (Partiya Dêmokrat a Kurdî li Sûriyê), also called el-Partî,[44] the Kurdish Democratic Progressive Party in Syria (Kurdish: Partiya Dîmoqratî Pêşverû Kurd li Sûriyê),[45] the Kurdish Socialist Party in Syria (Partiya Sosyalîst a Kurdî li Sûriyê),[46] the Kurdish

---

43 Vicken Cheterian, *Open Wounds: Armenians, Turks and a Century of Genocide* (New York: Oxford University Press, 2015), 150.

44 Sister party of the Iraqi Kurdish Democratic Party of Kurdistan (PDK) led by the Barzani family. The party split several times in the 1980s, but then unified with three other parties to form the new Democratic Party of Kurdistan (Kurdish: Partiya Demokrata Kurdistanê) in 2014, again acting as the sister party of Barzani's PDK.

45 Sister party of Jalal Talabani's Kurdish Patriotic Union of Kurdistan (PUK) in Iraq, which has been led by Abdulhamid Hadji Darwish since its founding in 1965.

46 This party, which existed from 1977 to 2002, was led by Muhammad Salih Gado, who aligned himself with the Kurdish Leftist Party in Syria in 2002, but then split from the latter and, with the Kurdish Leftist Party in Syria (Kurdish: Partiya Çep a Kurdî li Sûriyê), became part of the anti-PYD Kurdish National Council (ENKS) in 2011, before again breaking with the Council and returning to cooperating with the PYD.

Democratic Leftist Party (Partiya Çep a Demokrat a Kurdî li Sûriyê),[47] and some other breakaway groups—were primarily based in the Cizîrê. The latter was geographically much closer to the Iraqi Kurds, who, in turn, supported some of the Kurdish parties in Syria. Moreover, Qamişlo had become the intellectual and economic center for the Kurds.

The strongly rural Kurdish regions of Kobanê and Afrin were neglected by these parties. Even though the larger parties had some small groups in Afrin, their influence extended only to the urban upper class, while they had few followers among the population at large. The smaller parties were often not even represented in Afrin.

Thus, it was relatively easy for the PKK to build durable structures in Kobanê and Afrin that were tolerated by the regime. During the 1980s, the PKK dislodged the el-Partî, the Kurdish Leftist Party in Syria, and the other successor parties of the PDKS from Afrin. Though these parties never completely disappeared from the region, they had much less influence in Afrin than in the Cizîrê. The two Yekîtî parties founded in the 1990s and the newly unified PDKS (2014) are represented in the canton of Afrin today,[48] but they are weaker there than in the canton of Cizîrê.[49]

The PKK was not only able to plant roots in those peripheral areas that had hitherto not been at the center of Kurdish politics in Syria; it also banked on approaching new social strata. The parties that emerged from the historical PDKS were primarily an elite phenomenon. The social base of these parties consisted of academics, lawyers, businessmen, and large

---

47 This party split from the leftist wing of the Kurdish Democratic Party in Syria (Kurdish: Partiya Demokrat a Kurdî li Sûriyê [Çep]) in 1975, with which it then remerged in 2005 to form the Kurdish Freedom Party in Syria. The latter again split in 2011. The resulting splinter groups then formed the new PDK Syria (PDKS) with the sister party of the PDK (see note 44 above) and yet another splinter group in 2014.

48 In 1993, several smaller leftist parties merged into the Kurdish Democratic Unity Party in Syria (Kurdish: Partiya Yekîtîya Demokrat a Kurdî li Sûriyê [Yekîtî]) under Ismail Ammo. In 1999, the Kurdish Unity Party of Syria (Kurdish: Partiya Yekîtî ya Kurdî li Sûriyê) split from it, using "ya Kurdî" instead of "a Kurdî" in its party name and mentioning "Yekîtî" only once. In 2011, both were among the founding members of the Kurdish National Council (ENKS), but the Kurdish Democratic Unity Party in Syria (Yekîtî) left the Council and is now cooperating with the PYD, while the Kurdish Unity Party in Syria is now, together with the PDKS, the most important party in the ENKS, and thus the opposition to the PYD.

49 Schmidinger, *Krieg und Revolution in Syrisch-Kurdistan*, 110.

landowners. Until the 1980s, it was these strata that were involved in politics and received enough education to be able to develop national political demands based on their experience of discrimination as Kurds. As a revolutionary Marxist-Leninist party, the PKK relied on totally different social strata right from the start. Its goal was to revolutionize Kurdish society by approaching the masses on a completely different level: the impoverished and uneducated lower strata became the central target group for the party's agitation. Of course, students also participated as cadre in the PKK, but the actual target for building the party was the poorer and educationally alienated strata, which included not just ethnic Kurds, but, in the case of Afrin, also members of the Dūmī, who had an extremely marginal status in society quite similar to that of the Roma in Europe.

It is in the context of this twofold goal, the winning of a mass base and the revolutionizing of Kurdish society, that the purposeful political mobilization of the women should be seen. Feminist positions played an important role within the PKK right from the start and have always remained a central element of its ideology and propaganda, despite the sweeping ideological shift from Marxism-Leninism to eco-libertarian communalist positions. While it is true that the women in the PKK had to frequently fight back against relapses into patriarchal structures, it needs to be said that since its founding the PKK has represented the participation of women in all forms of political and military struggle as an important pillar of its policy, affirming the party's uncompromising struggle for the equality of women in Kurdish society.[50]

In Afrin women have been an important part of the PKK since the 1980s, both in its civil work in Syria and as fighters in Turkey. Since the beginning of the PKK's armed struggle, which was launched on August 15, 1984, with an assault on Turkish troops in Eruh and Şemdinli,[51] Syrian Kurdish women have fought in the ranks of the guerilla. Although young Kurdish women from Afrin have fought against the Turkish army since 1984, it must be said that these attacks were never launched from Afrin itself. Despite the hostility between Syria and Turkey, the Syrian-Turkish

50 Heidi Basch-Harod, "The Kurdish Women in Turkey: Nation Building and the Struggle of Gender Parity," in *Kurdish Awakening: Nation Building in a Fragmented Homeland*, ed. Ofra Bengio (Austin: University of Texas Press, 2014), 182.
51 Mehmet Akif Kumral, *Rethinking Turkey-Iraq Relations: The Dilemma of Partial Cooperation* (New York: Palgrave Macmillan, 2016), 122.

border itself has remained relatively quiet. The cross-border attacks by the PKK were launched from Iraq, where the party was able to build military bases after the Iraqi government lost control of parts of the Kurdish mountain regions during of the war with Iran.

Within Syria, the cooperation of the PKK with the regime did not mean that the newly won PKK mass base occupied itself exclusively with the Turkish Kurdish policy. For the regime, the PKK's armed struggle in Turkey had unintended consequences in Syria. In the 1980s, the Kurds, inspired by a newly gained self-confidence, began to celebrate the annual spring and New Year's festival of Newroz. When the regime prohibited these celebrations in 1986, this led to even more Kurds participating in them, giving the festival an even more pronounced political character. On March 21, 1986, thousands of young Kurds clad in traditional costumes came together in the Kurdish district of Damascus. When the police appeared and declared that it was forbidden to wear Kurdish festive dress, there were clashes. The security forces fired into the crowd, killing one young Kurd. His body was then brought back to his family in Qamişlo, where forty thousand people took part in his funeral, turning it into a political demonstration against the regime. In Afrin, as well, Kurdish youth took to the streets, with three Kurds killed and eighty arrested.[52]

At the end of the 1980s, the regime finally relaxed its control over Afrin and accorded the PKK, whose cooperation it felt sure of, greater political leeway in the region. This was in part because the regime was increasingly certain of its own stability and did not see the activities of the PKK as a danger to its own retention of power.

The regime permitted a number of independent candidates to run in the parliamentary elections in May 1990. As a result, some Kurdish deputies made their way into the Syrian parliament, even though they officially ran as "independents." In this respect, it is interesting to note that closer inspection clearly shows the political differences between the Cizîrê and Afrin. In the Cizîrê, three leading members of Kurdish parties that had emerged from the historical PDK were elected, while in Afrin six deputies from the ranks of the PKK were voted into parliament as independents.[53] With this, the PKK achieved an absolute dominance in the region of Afrin.

---

52 Vanly, "The Kurds in Syria and Lebanon," 128.
53 Jordi Tejel, *Syria's Kurds: History, Politics and Society* (London: Routledge, 2009), 67.

But the regional strength of the PKK in Afrin didn't change anything in the repressive Arab nationalist linguistic and cultural policy of the regime. Official education continued to be carried out exclusively in Arabic, and Kurdish publications, magazines, and radio continued to be forbidden. But even so, Kurdish publications circulated informally.[54] Those who respected the regime's red lines could carry out cultural work on an informal level. The illegal Kurdish parties organized Kurdish courses in private settings and published documents that circulated in limited numbers. All of this only reached small groups of intellectuals. Though the majority of the population could speak Kurdish and used the language in their daily lives, they often could not read and write Kurdish and were constrained to Arabic in their written communication.

From Hafiz to Bashar al-Assad

In the power struggle between Turkey and Syria in the second half of the 1990s, Syria turned out to be the weaker of the two. A central reason for this was the collapse of the Soviet Union, Syria's most important ally during the Cold War. Beginning in the 1970s, many Syrians had studied in Moscow, and there was close political, military, and economic cooperation between the two states. Without this partner, Syria was unable to hold its ground against Turkey in the long run. Moreover, in the 1990s, some of the big dam projects on the Euphrates were completed, leading to the very situation Damascus had feared from the beginning: Turkey now, metaphorically speaking, controlled Syria's water taps and could thus increase its pressure on Syria at will.

This pressure was further intensified in 1998 by Turkish troop concentrations in the border area. After a mediating effort by Egypt, Syria finally found itself forced to sign an agreement in Adana on October 20, 1998, that provided for the closure of the PKK training camps in Lebanon and the expulsion of Öcalan. From November 1998 to January 1999, Öcalan lived in Italy. On February 15, 1999, he was kidnapped in Kenya by the Turkish secret service, brought to Turkey, tried, and initially sentenced to death.

In Afrin, the abduction of Öcalan led to fierce protests by young PKK followers against the regime in February 1999. For the first time since 1986, PKK supporters in Afrin showed that they were no longer willing to

---

54   Alan George, *Syria: Neither Bread nor Freedom* (London: Zed Books, 2003), 125.

simply be instrumentalized against Turkey but were also ready to make demands of their own regime in Syria.

It is beyond the scope of this book to describe the consequences of Öcalan's abduction and show trial in detail. For the Syrian Kurds, the primary issue was that Öcalan's expulsion and later arrest ended the cooperation between the PKK and the Syrian state, and the party entered a period of severe crisis that led to an ideological and organizational reorientation in 2003.

During this period of crisis, there was yet another important event, namely, a change of government in Syria. Hafiz al-Assad, who had been severely ill with cancer for years, died on June 10, 2000. His son Bashar al-Assad, who had worked as an ophthalmologist in Great Britain up to that time, was brought back to Syria as his father's successor. At first, Bashar launched an—unfortunately short-lived—reform process that many observers called the "Damascus Spring." Political prisoners were released, and all of a sudden Syrian media was debating the future of the country with an openness hitherto unknown. Kurds, particularly from Qamişlo, also took part in these debates.

At the time, the PKK-dominated political scene in Afrin was still paralyzed by Öcalan's trial and the internal upheavals in its wake. But the base of the party was still intact, and in September 2003 it founded a new party, the Party of Democratic Union (Kurdish: Partiya Yekîtiya Demokrat, PYD), which unlike the PKK understood itself as an explicitly Syrian Kurdish party and made political demands of the Syrian state specifically on behalf of Syrian Kurds. The regime had already cracked down harshly on the PKK's grassroots base in the months before the founding of the party. In July 2003, it had even taken military action against PKK members in Afrin and other Kurdish regions and had handed Turkish party members arrested in the process over to the Turkish authorities. In subsequent years, the new party was often subjected to extremely harsh repressive state measures.

The relationship between the PYD and the PKK is fiercely discussed to this day. The PKK is regarded as a "terrorist organization" by the U.S. and parts of the EU,[55] while the armed forces founded by the PYD are

---

55 The PKK is on the list of the "Council Common Position of 27 December 2001 on the application of specific measures to combat terrorism," which is often simply called the "EU terror list," but how this is handled in practice varies

now the most important ally of the U.S. in Syria. Turkey regards all these groups as belonging to one and the same "terrorist organization." The relationship between the two parties is complex. There is no question that the PYD follows Abdullah Öcalan's ideology and is part of the larger PKK "party family" and the organizations friendly to it, a family that is organized in the Union of the Communities of Kurdistan (Kurdish: Koma Civakên Kurdistan, KCK), and that the party thus entertains close organizational ties to other "Apoist" parties, groups, and fronts.[56] All the same, the various organizations of the KCK are not identical and do not necessarily always pursue the same strategy. The reorganization of the PKK after 2000 from a centralist Marxist-Leninist cadre organization into a decentralized organization with a libertarian-communalist ideology, and the founding of the KCK in particular, was meant to give the individual member organizations more political leeway to act and react autonomously to different political situations.[57] The organizational models of the KCK member organizations and parties vary from state to state, and to some degree even from city to city. The PYD has thus been able to work

---

from EU state to EU state. While the approach to the PKK in Germany is very harsh, and some federal states even ban symbols of the PYD or the People's Protection Units (YPG) founded by the PYD and prosecute the possession of such symbols, in Austria the PKK is not subjected to harassment. On May 1, the PKK regularly marches under its own banner at the demonstration organized by the Socialist Party of Austria (SPÖ), until 2017 the federal chancellor's party. Parliamentarians of the SPÖ and the Greens regularly appear at the Newroz festival organized by the PKK-affiliated umbrella organization FEYKOM, and even the conservative ÖVP regularly sends a message of greetings that is read there. At the opening of an exhibition of photos from Syrian Kurdistan by the author of this book in the SPÖ's parliamentary club on November 23, 2016, then SPÖ club arbiter Andreas Schieder declared that the SPÖ not only regards the Turkish parliamentary Peoples' Democratic Party (Turkish: Halkların Demokratik Partisi) (HDP) as a sister party, but that this was also true for "the political arm of the PKK." Austria and many other EU member states do not persecute the various PKK front organizations or the party itself. The PKK is also not on the Consolidated United Nations Security Council Sanctions List, which is generally called the "UN terror list," meaning that the United Nations does not regard it as a terrorist organization.

56 "Apo" is a term of affection for Abdullah Öcalan. The ideology of the PKK and its sister organizations is therefore often called "Apoist."

57 Zeynep Kaya and Robert Lowe, "The Curious Question of the PYD-PKK Relationship," in *The Kurdish Question Revisited*, ed. Gareth Stansfield and Mohammed Shareef (London: Oxford University Press, 2017), 283.

as a Syrian Kurdish party in the same cultural-political milieu as other Syrian Kurdish parties.

During this initial stage, the PYD also had to struggle with internal conflicts that finally led to party splits. In 2004, the Kurdish Democratic United Party (Wifaq) had already broken away, and its founders Kamal Şahin and Kamuran Muhammad were murdered by PYD militants in February and August 2005, respectively. In September 2005, the third founder, Nadîm Yusif, fled his impending murder by the PYD, which accused the Wifaq Party of cooperating with the regime.[58] Also, in 2004, another group, the Democratic Reconciliation of the Syrian Kurds (Kurdish: Rêkeftina Demokrat a Kurdî ya Surî) under Fawzi Şingali, split from the PYD. After these initial conflicts, however, the party stabilized. It soon became the most important Kurdish opposition party in Syria and the heir of the 1980s and 1990s PKK.

The so-called soccer riots of March 2004 were not just the biggest Kurdish protests in Syria under Bashar al-Assad before 2011 but also once again demonstrated the political differences between the Cizîrê and Afrin. In March 2004, a soccer game in Qamişlo was accompanied by riots between Arab and Kurdish soccer fans. The brutal intervention of the Syrian regime cost the lives of nine Kurdish fans and led to protests in several cities in the Cizîrê, as well as in faraway Kobanê.[59]

That the situation in the Cizîrê escalated to this point also had to do with the fact that after the downfall of Saddam Hussein, the Kurds of the Cizîrê, who had close connections to Iraq, hoped to carve out an autonomous region in Syria similar to the one In Iraq, which was exactly what the regime that had just been described as part of the "Axis of Evil" by then U.S. president George W. Bush, feared—a development it wanted to prevent at all costs. But in Afrin, which remained largely insulated from the events in the Cizîrê, the situation remained relatively quiet. The new youth movements that emerged in the Cizîrê in 2004 never managed to establish roots in Afrin, which remained the key PKK area, and later a PYD area, as well as remaining firmly in the hands of the Syrian regime.

---

58 Michael M. Gunter, *Out of Nowhere: The Kurds of Syria in Peace and War* (London: Oxford University Press, 2014), 108.

59 Schmidinger, *Krieg und Revolution in Syrisch-Kurdistan*, 97ff.

The YPG and YPJ were the military forces in the region. The YPG introduced the draft in 2015, while the YPJ continued to be a voluntary army.

Syrian Troop Withdrawal in 2012

The protests against the Syrian regime likewise did not have Afrin as their point of departure. They began in the south of Syria and—as far as the Kurdish areas were concerned—once more in the Cizîrê, or to be more precise, in Amudê, where spontaneous protests against the regime began on March 27, 2011. The Kurdish mass protests against the regime in autumn also took place primarily in the towns of the Cizîrê, while the attitude in Afrin was initially cautious. Actually, the Arab opposition did not have much to offer the Kurds of Afrin. None of the Arab opposition alliances ever promised the Kurds more than "democracy." Like the government, all the relevant opposition forces rejected any form of federalism or the creation of an autonomous region for the Kurds.

In July 2012, when parts of Syria were already enmeshed in civil war, the regime and the PYD arrived at an agreement. Even though the precise contents of this accord remain unknown, between July 19 and July 24, the Syrian troops withdrew from the Kurdish settlement areas of Syria without a fight. On July 19, Kobanê, the hometown of Salih Muslim, the PYD party chair since 2010, was taken over by Kurdish units, and on the following day the Syrian army withdrew from Afrin. Thus, Afrin has not been under the control of the Syrian army and the Syrian police forces since July 20, 2012. The situation in the Cizîrê is different. While the regime retained its presence in parts of the major town of Qamişlo, as well as in the provincial capital of al-Hasaka (Kurdish: Hesîçe), its withdrawal from Afrin was complete. The whole region was thereafter administered by the PYD from July 2012 until the Turkish attack in 2018.

For the security of the areas newly taken over, the PYD founded the People's Protection Units (Kurdish: Yekîneyên Parastina Gel, YPG) and the Women's Protection Units (Kurdish: Yekîneyên Parastina Jin, YPJ), which were assembled by experienced cadre of the People's Protection Forces (Hêzên Parastina Gel, HPG), the PKK guerilla army, under its commander Murat Karayılan. Before their commitment to the YPG, both its highest commander Sîpan Hemo and its speaker Rêdûr Xelîl were top Halkların Demokratik Partisi (HDP) commanders in Qendîl, and it is known that both still coordinate important decisions with the HDP headquarters there. The same is also true for Nesrîn Abdalla, the highest commander of the YPJ. The takeover and provision of security in the region by the YPG and the YPJ opened a new chapter in the history of Afrin. For the first time since the end of the rule of the Mendî and the centralization of the Ottoman Empire, the Kurds were administering themselves.

Democratic Confederalism
in the Canton of Afrin

With the withdrawal of the Syrian army, the Kurds gained the opportunity to administer their region themselves. Since the PYD had been the dominant force in the region since before 2012, it was easier for the party in Afrin than it was in the Cizîrê to take de facto state power and build a Kurdish para-state that was meant to function according to the principles of "democratic confederalism," as they had been formulated by Abdullah Öcalan in the 2000s on the basis of theories of Murray Bookchin and other eco-anarchists.

Under this administration, from 2012 to 2018, Afrin represented one of the safest regions of Syria and served as a refuge for hundreds of thousands of internally displaced people from other parts of Syria, including many Arabs from Aleppo. However, Turkey's attack at the end of January 2018 destroyed this haven.

Administration and Politics

From the perspective of the Syrian government, the region of Afrin is a district (*manṭiqat*) of the province of Aleppo and consists in turn of seven subdistricts (*nāḥiyah*, plural: *nawāḥī*). From the perspective of Kurdish self-administration, the canton of Afrin and the canton of Shaba together form the region of Afrin. The canton of Afrin is in turn divided into the three regions, Afrin (Efrîn), Cindirês, and Reco.

After the withdrawal of the government troops in 2012, the Kurdish parties in Syria initially tried to build a joint administration in the Kurdish areas. A few days before the army's withdrawal, on July 11, 2012, the "People's Councils" propagated by the PYD and the Kurdish National

THE BATTLE FOR THE MOUNTAIN OF THE KURDS

Council in Syria (Kurdish: Encûmena Niştimanî ya Kurdî li Sûriyeyê, ENKS) met in the Iraqi Kurdish capital of Erbil and agreed on the creation of a Supreme Kurdish Committee (Kurdish: Desteya Bilind a Kurd). The latter was meant to serve as a kind of transitional government, but that never really worked, and it was haunted by a permanent conflict between the PYD and the ENKS. Locally, this conflict played a more important role in the Cizîrê than in it did in Afrin, the latter being dominated by the PYD, in any case. Compared to the situation in the Cizîrê, the parties of the ENKS had only a marginal position in Afrin. After lengthy negotiations between the PYD and the ENKS, during which the PYD used its armed forces to shape the reality on the ground in Afrin and worked to create a legislative council that functioned as a government, the autonomous canton of Afrin was proclaimed on January 2, 2014.

The new Legislative Council had 101 members, including representatives of the Alevi and Êzîdî religious minorities, as well as representatives of the Arab Emirati and Bobeni tribes. On the local level, a council system was formed, stipulating a female quota of 40 percent.

The concept of "democratic confederalism"—far-reaching self-government on a municipal and communal level—is based not on an ethnic but on a strictly territorial autonomy and, at least theoretically, on strong decentralization. The commune is thus simultaneously the smallest unit and the center of social organization. Each commune is supported by a Mala Gel (People's House), which, among other things, serves as a form of first-instance jurisdiction.[1] Building on this, councils are first integrated on the level of a village or a city district, then on a regional level, and finally on the canton level. Within these councils, certain committees are responsible for certain areas of politics. The councils' decisions are normally based on consensus.

Similar council systems have been used on numerous occasions in the course of revolutionary history. For example, councils were created during the Spanish Civil War and the Russian Revolution ("soviet" means council in Russian). In Austria, as well, workers and soldiers' councils were formed in 1918 and contributed to launching the revolutionary process that ended the Habsburg monarchy. Bavaria and Hungary both

---

1   Anja Flach, Ercan Ayboğa, and Michael Knapp, *Revolution in Rojava: Frauenbewegung und Kommunalismus zwischen Krieg und Embargo* (Hamburg: VSA: Verlag, 2015), 109.

saw the creation of revolutionary council republics at the end of World War I. Today we find similar political initiatives in the council system of the Mexican Zapatistas and, to come back to our area, in Rojava, or West Kurdistan, which is how the Syrian Kurds refer to this region. Council systems are different from a parliamentary democracy in that they don't delegate political power to a parliament or deputies, instead political action is carried out by the directly elected councils: individual members of the councils cannot act freely and can be removed from their positions by the electorate at any time should they fail to respect the will of the voters.

In a council system, the voters are primarily organized on the local level and elect workplace representatives, as well as city district or village representatives. The councils thus elected in turn send some of their members as delegates to the next superordinate organizational level. At least in theory, the political decisions are always made on the local level. The superordinate councils on the regional or the federal level have to regularly coordinate their decisions with the local levels. Ideally, this leads to a system of direct democracy in which the individual members of the councils merely carry out the will of their voters, instead of ruling over them. This ideological turnaround of the PKK and its sister organizations in the first few years of the 2000s was based on the theories of U.S. eco-anarchists, such as Murray Bookchin and Janet Biehl. Based on these theories, structures were created in Afrin that transferred many daily administrative decisions to the local level.

Just as in the whole PKK sphere of influence, gender politics plays an important role in Rojava. On all political levels, the so-called Hevserok system has been realized, which a publication close to the party describes in the following way: "Whether in a municipal administration, in a court, or elsewhere—coordination is always shared by two persons, one of whom is a woman."[2]

In practical terms, however, all council systems inevitably pose the question of whether the councils are really the only decision-making institution or if important decision are not actually taken by other bodies with less democratic legitimization. Thus, in the early Soviet Union there was a major conflict between anarchists and council communists, on the one hand, and party communists, on the other. The anarchists and council

---

2   Ibid., 123.

The building housing the bodies responsible for the self-administration of the canton of Afrin, including Prime Minister Hêvî Îbrahîm Mustefa's office.

communists demanded "All power to the councils" and accused the politicians of the Communist Party of having given all power to the party. Particularly in situations of civil war, such as in the early Soviet Union, but also in Syria, military logic often gains the upper hand in decisive strategic questions, and, concomitantly, the military structure acquires a growing importance in comparison to the direct democratic councils.

This basic problem for council systems and democracy in situations of war is also present in the self-administered Kurdish regions in Syria. Parallel to the council system, the military units of the People's Protection Units (YPG) and the Women's Protection Units (YPJ) certainly also represent important sites of power.

The PYD also continues to be a site of power. Even though most member parties of the Kurdish National Council (ENKS) have boycotted the new system to this day, the PYD succeeded in wooing some smaller leftist parties away from the ENKS and in convincing some additional parties to participate in the council system. In Afrin, this is primarily the Kurdish Democratic Unity Party in Syria (Yekîtî). This party, founded in 1993 as a merger of three leftist parties, is led by founding member and chairman

Ismail Ammo and is one of the most active parties in Syrian Kurdistan.[3] Though it was a founding member of the ENKS, since its exclusion from that body in December 2014, it represents the most important system-immanent opposition in Afrin. Unlike most other parties, its secretary general of many years, Mihyedîn Şêx Alî, does not come from the Cizîrê but from Afrin itself. This might also have contributed his party turning its back on the ENKS parties in the Cizîrê and participating in the PYD's self-administration. Mihyedîn Şêx Alî's Democratic Unity Party is not the only former ENKS party to have left the National Council to join the PYD's administration, but it is the only one that has activists working in Afrin.

The second party represented in Afrin, the Democratic Party of Kurdistan in Syria (Partiya Demokrata Kurdistan a Sûriye, PDKS), even in its post-2014 reunited form, continues to represent the heart of the Kurdish National Council and remains strictly opposed to the PYD. When the intra-Kurdish conflict between the PYD and the PDKS grew more intense, the party offices of the latter were closed down in all three cantons. The PDKS's party chairman Abdelrehman Apo was arrested several times, most recently on July 7, 2017, and has yet to be released. To all intents and purposes, his party has been unable to do political work in Afrin since his arrest.

Until 2016, there was no official joint administration of Kurdish areas above the level of the cantons. The Democratic Federation of North Syria-Rojava (Kurdish: Federasyona Demokratîk a Bakurê Sûriyê û Rojava) was announced only on March 17, 2016, with the canton of Afrin becoming a part of it. It was rechristened the Democratic Federation of North Syria (Kurdish: Federaliya Demokratîk a Bakûrê Sûriyê) in December 2017. The renaming was meant to replace the explicit reference to the Kurds and with a more ethnically neutral name to address the ever-expanding Arabic-speaking areas that the PYD was able to wrestle from Islamic State control in 2017.

From January 2014 to 2017, the canton of Afrin formed a unit, and the areas around Tal Rifaat, conquered in 2016 during the race to establish a connection between the Kurdish areas, were integrated into it. But at the

---

3   Bekir Halhalli, "Kurdish Political Parties in Syria: Past Struggles and Future Expectations," in *Comparative Kurdish Politics in the Middle East: Actors, Ideas, and Interests*, ed. Emel Elir Tugdar and Serhun Al (New York: Palgrave Macmillan, 2018), 38.

end of July 2017, a local government reform was introduced that divided the Democratic Federation into three regions with six cantons.[4] The new region of Afrin was divided into two cantons. The canton of Afrin (Kurdish: Kantona Efrînê) consists of the Kurdish core region that had constituted the old canton of Afrin from 2012 to 2016, before the areas around Tal Rifaat were conquered. The linguistically mixed area of Tal Rifaat became the canton of Shabha (Kurdish: Kantona Şehbayê), which also includes the areas around Manbij (west of the Euphrates) that are not directly connected with the areas around Tal Rifaat. The new canton of Afrin was itself divided into the three districts Afrin (Efrîn), Cindirês, and Reco.

From the beginning, the Alevi and PYD member Hêvî Îbrahîm Mustefa from Afrin served as prime minister of the canton of Afrin (and later, region). The deputy prime ministers were Remzi Şêxmus and Ebdil Hemîd Mistefa. What follows is a complete list of ministers:

Minister of Foreign Affairs: Silêman Ceefer
Minister of Defense: Ebdo Îbrahîm
Minister of the Interior: Parêzer Hesen Beyrem
Minister of Finance: Remezan Elî
Minister of Justice: Seîd Esmet Xûbarî
Minister of Planning: Nûrşan Hisên
Minister of Labor and Social Security: Erîfe Bekir
Minister of Education: Riyaz Menle Mehemed
Minister of Energy: Kamîran Ehmed Şefîi Bilal
Minister of Agriculture: Eyûb Mihemed
Minister of Health: Xelîl Şêx Hesen
Minister of Economy and Trade: Ehmed Yûsif
Minister for the Families of Martyrs: Ebdilhenan Şêxo
Minister of Culture: Hêvîn Şêxo
Minister of Transport: Welîd Selame
Minister of Youth and Sports: Fazil Robcî
Minister of History and Tourism: Reşîd Ehmed
Minister of Religious Affairs: Mihemed Hemîd Qasim
Minister of Women's and Family Affairs: Fatme Lekto

---

4   Thomas Schmidinger, "Militärische Expansion mit US-Unterstützung: Aktuelle Entwicklungen in Syrisch-Kurdistan," in *Wiener Jahrbuch für Kurdische Studien 5: Sprache—Migration—Zusammenhalt: Kurdisch und seine Diaspora*, ed. Katharina Brizić et al. (Vienna: Praesens Verlag, 2017), 239.

The author presenting his 2014 book on Syrian Kurdistan and a box of Mozart balls to Prime Minister Hêvî Îbrahîm Mustefa at her office in the city of Afrin.

Minister of Human Rights: Xelîl Sîno
Minister of Supervision: Etûf Ebdo
Minister of Information: Ebdil Rehman Selman

Finally, in the second half of 2017, elections took place under difficult circumstances. Municipal elections were held in the entire Democratic Federation of North Syria on September 22. They were boycotted by the ENKS, but in Afrin, apart from the PYD and its allies, candidates of the Kurdish Democratic Unity Party in Syria (Yekîtî) and the Syrian National Democratic Alliance, an association of Arab parties, also participated, as did a number of independent candidates.

At the December 1, 2017, regional elections, three different lists presented themselves in Afrin: the Democratic Nation (Kurdish: Lîsta Netewa Demokratîk, LND) list included the ruling PYD and a number of smaller opposition parties. While in the Cizîrê, it is primarily the two Christian-Assyrian allies of the PYD, Ishow Gowriye's Suroyo Union Party and Ninos Isho's Assyrian Democratic Party, that play a political role, these parties are not present in Afrin, as there is no Assyrian population there. The other mini-parties, the LND, the Kurdish Leftist Party in Syria (Partiya Çep a Kurdî li Sûriyê), the Modernity and Democracy Party of

Syria (Kurdish: Partiya Nûjen û Demokratîk li Sûriyeyê), the Green Party of Kurdistan (Kurdish: Partiya Kesk a Kurdistanê), the Liberal Party of Kurdistan (Kurdish: Partiya Lîberal a Kurdistanê), and a few other splinter groups, have no presence in Afrin. Thus, in Afrin this alliance basically consisted of the PYD alone.

The most important system-immanent opposition in Afrin was the Kurdish Democratic Unity Party in Syria (Yekîtî), which in the Cizîrê ran as part of an electoral alliance, the Kurdish National Alliance in Syria (Kurdish: Hevbendiya Niştimanî a Kurdî li Sûriyê). But in Afrin, the other parties in this alliance were de facto non-existent, so the party simply ran under its own name in that region.

The third list, the Syrian National Democratic Alliance, is a multi-ethnic alliance of small opposition parties that are mostly Arab allies of the PYD.

In the end, the PYD-dominated LND was the clear winner with 89.8 percent of the votes. The LND won 1,056 of an aggregate of 1,176 mandates. As for the Kurdish Democratic Unity Party in Syria (Yekîtî), with 6.12 percent and 72 seats, it managed to do much better than in the other two regions, and the Syrian National Democratic Alliance was also able to win 8 seats with 0.68 percent of the vote. Another 40 mandates (3.4 percent) went to independent candidates.

However, given the electoral boycott by the ENKS parties, the result of the elections confers only a limited democratic legitimacy. But given the conditions in many other parts of Syria, merely holding elections that allowed for (albeit system-immanent) opposition is, nonetheless, an important achievement. Since Afrin has been a traditional PKK strong-hold since the 1980s, it is quite likely that the PYD would have won a major-ity in Afrin even if all relevant political forces had participated in the elections and would surely have done better than in the Cizîrê under such conditions, but in truly democratic elections with all forces running it would certainly not have won 90 percent of the vote and the mandates.

Therefore, even though the situation in Afrin is more democratic and pluralist than in those areas of Syria that are either under the rule of the totalitarian regime or under the rule of jihadist and political Islamist militias, it is not democratic in the narrower sense of the word. The state of siege that Afrin was subjected to by various militias, the Turkish government, and the regime created a situation that tended to prevent a further democratization of the region. For most of the inhabitants of

Afrin, however, it was important to be able to defend their reasonably peaceful civilian existence, and this they managed to do until January 2018.

Economy

Because of its winter rain and fertile soil, Afrin has been an important agrarian region for centuries. It is only during the summer months that conditions are so dry that gardens must be irrigated if they are to be cultivated. Pomegranate, citrus fruits, almonds, grapes, and other types of fruit are grown in the region. In addition, cotton is cultivated on the plain south of the city of Afrin. Since antiquity, the region has been particularly known for its olive orchards, which, according to some sources, include up to twenty-six million trees. Olives and olive oil from Afrin have always been recognized in Syria for their high quality, including as an export product. Many of the olive trees are centuries old. It is even said that some of the particularly long-lived trees were planted by the Romans. And, indeed, there probably has been a continuity in the cultivation of olives stretching from antiquity to the present.

For centuries, the olive oil of Afrin was exported to Aleppo, where it was used, among other things, for the production of the famous Aleppo soap that is exclusively made of olive and laurel oil and was even exported to Europe's organic grocery stores. Because of the civil war in Aleppo, since 2012 some of this soap production has been transferred to Afrin. Other industries based in Aleppo were also transferred to Afrin because of the fighting. If one wandered through the city of Afrin in 2015, one would see a busy town with a number of newly constructed buildings and small or medium-size enterprises. For example, the textile industry developed into one of the most important branches of business in the region. In 2016, Afrin had four hundred textile plants with seventeen thousand employees that sold their products throughout Syria.[5]

It is also in this region that an Armenian family business used to produce Syria's best and most famous Arak (aniseed brandy). Until 2018, spirits of all sorts were available in Afrin, although they were much more expensive than had previously been the case, because the transportation was often quite laborious.

---

5   "Rojava: The Economic Branches in Detail," *Co-operation in Mesopotamia*, June 2016, accessed September 30, 2018, https://mesopotamia.coop/rojava-the-economic-branches-in-detail/.

The first two winters after the withdrawal of the Syrian army were very hard in all three Kurdish regions of Syria. There was hardly any fuel available, and people often queued for hours in front of the bakeries. I still remember well the sight of people chopping up their furniture for firewood. In the winter of 2013–2014, I saw chilblains on the feet of a small child from a family of internally displaced people, the first I had ever seen. Power supply was limited to just a few hours per day, and medical care was disastrous. However, by 2015, the worst of these supply problems had largely been solved. The collapse of Syria's highly centralized and state-run economy led to a war economy in which the various warring parties traded with each other even though they were enemies on the battlefield.

Ultimately, Afrin succeeded in largely restoring the power and water supply. But even so, right up until the Turkish invasion, fuel was much more problematic than in the Kurdish regions further to the east, which have been able to supply themselves from the oil wells in the Cizîrê. Afrin, on the other hand, had to rely on the Syrian fuel market, meaning that the gas and diesel prices were about ten times as high as in Kobanê and the Cizîrê.

Strategically important goods, such as water or electricity, that had been distributed by the Syrian state until 2012 had effectively been taken over by the PYD, and, since 2014, by the canton and region of Afrin. Nonetheless, the salaries of state officials were in part paid by the regime right to the end, although there were problems with the disbursement and remittance of the salaries.

By 2018, there was no longer any regular banking system in Afrin. The Syrian lira (often also called the pound), which continued to be the medium of exchange, underwent pronounced inflation during the Syrian civil war. In 2016, inflation reached 43.9 percent, and in 2017 increased by an additional 25.5 percent.[6] International remittances were only possible via the hawala system so widespread in the Islamic world. In this system, somebody, say, in Europe, pays a trusted person a sum of money, which will then be paid out in, say, Syria by another trusted person. For the most part, the "hawaladars," the "trusted persons" in this system, are family members located in various regions whose confidence in one another

---

6   Central Intelligence Agency, "The World Factbook," 2017, accessed September 30, 2018, https://www.cia.gov/library/publications/the-world-factbook/fields/2092.html.

The police forces of the canton of Afrin included female police officers.

is based on family membership. In the case of Afrin, the money was for the most part never physically transferred to Syria. A telephone call to the hawaladar in Afrin was sufficient to prompt the latter to pay out the required sum on the same day. In Afrin, this role was assumed by the Haftaro family, which in recent years became one of the wealthiest families of Afrin as a result.

Authors close to the PYD have frequently highlighted the cooperatives in Rojava as an alternative to capitalism. In fact, using front-end financing, the canton of Afrin promoted cooperatives, particularly for women. Women's cooperatives also played an important role in the PYD's sociopolitical model, seeking to enable women to earn an income independent of their husbands. Many of these women's cooperatives were either directly created by the PYD's political organizations or its front organizations or were strongly supported by them. Thus, the women's Inanna cooperative, producing onions, garlic, beans, and chickpeas, which was founded in November 2016, was launched with the help of the PYD women's organization Kongreya Star.[7] As important as the coop-

---

7   "Inanna: A Women's Agricultural Coop in Afrin," *Co-operation in Mesopotamia*, accessed September 30, 2018, https://mesopotamia.coop/inanna-a-womens-agricultural-coop-in-afrin/.

After the withdrawal of the Syrian army from Afrin in 2012, portraits of Bashar al-Assad were destroyed and bilingual place-name signs in Kurdish and Arabic were installed.

eratives may have been for the women participating in them, it should be clearly understood that these cooperatives were not for the most part pillars of Afrin's economy, and only a relatively small number of people worked in cooperatives.

Overall, until the war with Turkey the supply situation in Afrin was relatively good despite the isolation of the area. All essential goods were available in Afrin, even though the prices were frequently excessive. The only problems were with specialized medicines or machines, which were impossible to get. The initial problems with the export of olives and other agrarian products had largely been solved in the previous years. Trade with the areas under the control of the Syrian government had markedly improved since the end of the blockade of Nubl and az-Zahrā', and, until 2018, there had also been trade with the areas controlled by Sunni Arab opposition militias.

Education and Academia

When Afrin was taken over by the PYD in 2012, the Syrian regime didn't close down all civilian institutions in Afrin immediately. Initially, officials and teachers remained on the payroll of the regime, and the schools continued to teach in Arabic using the Syrian curriculum. Until 2015, the new Kurdish authorities limited themselves to offering Kurdish-language courses in addition to the Arabic instruction run by the Syrian state. But in 2015–2016, Kurdish instruction was introduced in the three cantons. After that, in Afrin, all Kurdish students were taught using the Kurdish and Latin alphabets, with the first three years of school instruction exclusively in Kurdish. From the fourth grade foreign-language instruction in Arabic and English was added. However, Arabic schools were still available for the Arab children of the region.

August 2015 finally saw the inauguration of the first Kurdish university in Syria, the University of Afrin (Kurdish: Zanîngeha Efrînê), mainly staffed by former professors of the University of Aleppo. The University of Afrin opened one year before a second Kurdish university in Qamişlo but, like all other Kurdish institutions, was not recognized by the Syrian state. Nevertheless, the university has been making an important contribution to higher education in the region, particularly because, due to the developments in Aleppo since 2012, the students from Afrin have been studying in very dangerous conditions.

In the first year of study, the university only offered three courses: electronics, Kurdish language and literature, and economics. "Kurdish Language and Literature" also aimed to prepare Kurdish teachers to meet the urgent need created by the conversion of education to Kurdish. In 2016, courses in medicine, journalism, and agriculture were added. Even though initially only the most pressing courses of study were offered, it was always the goal of the university's energetic team to eventually become a full-fledged university that would also offer doctoral programs and other branches of study.

During the period when I was in contact with the university, management representatives also displayed an interest in international exchanges, which, however, proved to be very difficult to organize because of Afrin's isolation and the university's lack of state accreditation. International academic contact was basically limited to personal relations with individual scholars, including the author of this book. For a university without official state recognition in a region surrounded by war, participating in official exchange programs or joint research projects is, of course, almost impossible. Had Afrin not been attacked by Turkey in 2018, the university could have developed into an important regional research and teaching center, and in time formed links with the international academic community. But with the beginning of the Turkish bombardment of the city of Afrin, teaching had to be ended in March 2018.

Safe Haven for the Internally Displaced

Nobody knows exactly how many displaced people from Aleppo and other war-torn parts of Syria arrived in Afrin in recent years, but the number might well be close to three hundred thousand. Kurds from Aleppo were often given refuge and support by their relatives. But Arabs and members of other minorities were also taken in. If nothing else, those who came to Afrin with absolutely no money were provided with a tent and a safe haven.

In February 2015, I had the opportunity to visit one of the tent camps of the destitute refugees from Aleppo. At the time, thirty Arab families who had fled the contested town of Aleppo in 2013 were being hosted in the Robar Camp, near the village Basilê. The village of Basilê is located on the plateau of the Ğabal Simʿān. The tent camp was located further into the plateau and only seven kilometers [four and a half miles] from the regime enclave Nubl and az-Zahrāʾ, with the jihadist Jabhat al-Nusra on the other side. The tents were guarded by an approximately seventy-year-old inhabitant of Basilê, who sat in a small shack in front of an oil stove throughout the night with a Kalashnikov in case of an emergency. This was not because the Kurds were afraid of their Arab guests, but because the front line was not far away, the mountains are lonely, and the villagers felt in some way responsible for the security of their guests. Zaki Sultane—the elderly guard—had himself only returned from Aleppo to his village when the civil war began. In Aleppo, he had owned a small shawarma restaurant that eventually came to be located at the front line separating the rebels from the regime, so he decided to return to his former village and his relatives.

The refugees, with whom I was allowed to talk uninterrupted and unsupervised, were by and large satisfied with their situation. They were certainly grateful that the Kurds had taken them in, allowing them to escape the war, at least for the time being, but they would still have preferred to be in the city. The children were poorly dressed and received only very rudimentary schooling. Each day, the men tried to take the bus to Afrin to work as day laborers. The camp had no regular supply of money, clothing, or food, so this was how the men tried to make ends meet for their families. They also told me that sometimes the trip to Afrin proved vain, and they ended up spending money for the bus and not earning anything. However, they did frequently find work at one of the many construction sites. The next day, I did, in fact, see some of the men in Afrin at the edge of the main square, waiting with other Arab men to be hired by someone for some odd job.

Some of the women had had terrible war experiences involving sexual violence, and some of the men also struck me as psychologically distraught. Almost nobody in the camp saw any future for themselves. None of them had money for smugglers to take them to Europe. The thirty families were stuck in this tent camp, glad to have escaped the war but without any hope of leading a genuinely decent life in the foreseeable future. There were no international aid organizations present, and the Kurdish authorities were visibly overwhelmed by the thousands of internally displaced people. But even so, at least civilians were not turned away.

For these people and thousands of others, Afrin was a precarious haven. The war was never far away, and people were living from hand to mouth, but they were at least safe from violence and able to survive, and the children could get a rudimentary education. This alone was more than was available in other parts of Syria. Many of the internally displaced who had found refuge in Afrin between 2012 and 2018 are now again on the road, this time with the Kurdish inhabitants of Afrin, who have now also been expelled.

Development of the Canton
of Afrin from 2012 to 2018

History did of course not come to a standstill with the declaration of autonomy for Afrin. At any rate, in the five and a half years of Kurdish autonomy in Afrin, history was written as far as the development of Syria and Kurdistan is concerned, a history that cannot be separated from the evolution of the Syrian civil war.

It is beyond the scope of a book about Afrin to try to reconstruct the genesis of the Syrian civil war. What is important for Afrin, though, is the fact that this conflict, which is the result of a brutal overreaction of the regime to the protests and the militarization of the resistance into a civil war that has led to far-reaching change over the last seven years. In 2011, the armed opposition initially came from Syrian army deserters who refused the regime's orders to fire on protesters. They saw themselves primarily as defenders of the civilian protests, while also defending themselves against their former fellow soldiers, who were expected to use force and violence against deserters. It was the decision of Turkey, Saudi Arabia, Qatar, and Kuwait to arm the opposition militias, on the one hand, and Russia and Iran's military support for the regime, on the other hand, that accelerated the militarization of the conflict, which became an open civil war in many areas of Syria in 2012. In a sense, after the withdrawal of the government army the Kurdish areas established themselves as a neutral third party. Though some of the Kurdish parties sympathized to various degrees with the Syrian opposition, the PYD in particular initially tried to remain on the sidelines of the war and to focus on the Kurdish areas.

The city of Afrin is the only urban center in the region. Locals and refugees from other parts of Syria mingle in the city park.

Autonomy with Difficult Neighbors

During the second half of 2012, various jihadist groups gained increasing strength within the opposition. This was particularly true of Jabhat al-Nusra, the Syrian branch of al-Qaeda, which beginning in the spring of 2013 broke with the so-called Islamic State in Iraq and Sham (Greater Syria). After the proclamation of the caliphate in June 2014, the latter simplified its name to the Islamic State. At the same time, apart from the so-called Free Syrian Army (Arabic: al-Jaish as-Sūrī al-hurr), which was never unified but was a conglomerate of various local armed opposition groups formed in 2012 by a number of Salafist militias and militias close to the Muslim Brotherhood, the local jihadist militia, Ahrar ash-Sham, was established in 2011, and between 2012 and November 2013 it formed the Syrian Islamic Front (Arabic: al-Jabha al-Islāmiyya as-Sūriyya) with other political Islamic militias. In September 2012, the Saudi financed Syrian Islamic Liberation Front (Arabic: Tahrīr Sūriyā al-Islāmīya) was founded, and, on the Kurdish side, in early 2013, a Kurdish Islamic Front with around one thousand fighters came together, primarily focused on the struggle against the PYD.

In September 2013, the Free Syrian Army, which was initially regarded as a pro-Western opposition army but always lacked a joint chain of command, finally split: the political Islamic forces within the FSA organized a coalition with jihadist groups, including Ahrar ash-Sham and Jabhat al-Nusra, and expelled the secular units of the FSA from the north of Syria following a brief civil war.[1] In autumn 2014, a number of secular revolutionaries who had fled to Turkey returned to Syria to side with the YPG, to help the Kurds to defend Kobanê against the Islamic State.

The latter, however, primarily posed a threat to the Kurdish areas farther to the east. Afrin was only confronted with the so-called Islamic State in Iraq and Sham from October 2013 to February 2014, when the latter succeeded in taking control of the town of A'zaz, directly to the east of Afrin. But it was finally expelled on February 28 by a very broad alliance consisting of the so-called Northern Storm Brigade (Arabic: Liwa Asifat al-Shamal), Jabhat al-Nusra, and the Kurdish Jabhat al-Akrad, in coopera-tion with the YPG.

Afrin primarily had its military conflicts with Jabhat al-Nusra and Ahrar ash-Sham, and these were limited to occasional skirmishes early in the civil war. For example, in July 2013, the Êzîdî village Basûfanê came under attack. But until 2018, there were no serious attempts to conquer Afrin. At the same time, Afrin played a mediating role between the Shiite militias loyal to the regime in Nubl and az-Zahrā', which had been isolated from July 2012 to February 2016, and the moderate opposition. Since the only access to Turkey was via the Öncüpınar border crossing between A'zaz and Kilis, the Kurdish authorities in Afrin tried to come to some agreement with the political Islamic militias present in A'zaz. In this case, it was the fighters of Jabhat al-Akrad who played a certain mediating role between the factions. This Kurdish militia had been part of the FSA until its expulsion in August 2013 but had remained in the linguistically mixed region around A'zaz to protect the Kurdish villages and for a long time functioned as local mediators between the Kurds and the Arab opposition in the region.

Even though the relationship between the YPG and the militias sta-tioned around A'zaz between 2014 and 2015—Jabhat al-Nusra, Liwa al-Tawhid, and Harakat Nur ad-Din az-Zanki—was by no means friendly, the two sides communicated and maintained some sort of functioning cross-border traffic. Everyone from A'zaz who wanted to enter the canton

---

1   Since that time, secular Arab opposition militias acting under the banner of the FSA have only been present in the south of Syria, at the border with Jordan.

A checkpoint in February 2015 near the village Qestelê between the canton of Afrin and the area around A'zaz, ruled by Ahrar al-Sham and Jabhat al-Nusra at the time. Everyone entering the Kurdish territory was searched for fear of terrorist attacks.

of Afrin had to show their passport and agree to be searched by YPG/YPJ fighters at one of the checkpoints near the villages Qestelê and Qitmê. Vehicles and baggage were also checked to prevent people from bringing in bombs and explosives. Essentially, these checkpoints acted as border controls between the areas under the control of the Arab Sunni opposition militias and those under the control of the YPG.

In 2015, walls and small circular brick guardhouses were erected at the border of Afrin, and until the end the year almost uninterrupted border fortification was carried out along the demarcation line between the YPG and the Sunni-Arab militias. In the north, Turkey erected a much higher border wall. Turkey's wall consists of concrete blocks that are two meters [six feet] wide, three meters [nine feet] high, and weigh seven tons and is equipped with barbed wire.[2] Afrin was thus closed in from the north and the west, and the smuggling of medicine and other important

---

2   "Grenzmauer zwischen der Türkei und Syrien," *TRT Deutsch*, December 18, 2017, accessed September 30, 2018, http://www.trt.net.tr/deutsch/turkei/ 2017/12/18/grenzmauer-zwischen-der-turkei-und-syrien-870775.

goods across the green border that had been so widespread until then became basically impossible.

The Battle against the Islamic State and the Race with Turkey

Just as in the east of the Kurdish area, in Afrin, the YPG and the YPJ actively participated in the new umbrella organization, the Syrian Democratic Forces (Qūwāt Sūriyā ad-dīmuqrāṭīya, Hêzên Sûriya Demokratîk, SDF), which were founded on October 10, 2015, and represented an important precondition for closer military and political cooperation with the U.S. against the so-called Islamic State, or IS. Apart from the Kurdish units of the YPG, YPJ, and Jabhat al-Akrad (Kurdish: Enîya Kurdan), the SDF also includes the Turkmen Battalion of the Northern Sun (Katā'ib Shams ash-Shimāl), the Arab Army of Revolutionaries (Jaish aṭ-Ṭūwār),[3] the Quwāt aṣ-Ṣanādīd militia deployed by the Arab tribe of the Shammar, the Military Council of the Suryoye, which had merged with the YPG in 2014, and several other smaller secular units that came out of the former Free Syrian Army. Despite the continued military and political dominance of the YPG and the YPJ, the SDF represented the ecumenical alliance that the U.S. had time and again spercified as a precondition for military support. The U.S. government was thus able to claim to its NATO ally Turkey that it was not directly supporting the YPG/YPJ, but rather a broader military alliance.[4]

While this alliance led to massive territorial gains to the detriment of the IS in the east of Syria, in Afrin it actually only started to play a role in 2016, when the IS attempted to carve a corridor between Kobanê and Afrin and, at the same time, to win the race to control the area of interest to the Kurds, Turkey and its allies, and the Syrian regime. This area, which at the beginning of the year had been largely under the IS control, also included a corridor from the Turkish border near A'zaz to Aleppo used by various pro-Turkish Sunni Arab and Turkmen rebel groups, while the Kurds, for their part, would have been able to connect their separate areas by conquering this stretch of land. When, on February 3, 2016, the regime broke the siege around the Shia enclave of Nubl and az-Zahrā', connecting

---

3   This, in turn, is a merger of several former secular FSA brigades that had largely been expelled from their original regions by the political Islamic brigades of the former FSA and their jihadist allies in September and October 2013.

4   Thomas Schmidinger, *Rojava*, (Vienna: Mandelbaum, 2016), 141.

the enclave with the government-held part of Aleppo and simultaneously cutting off the rebel area of A'zaz from that in Aleppo, a race over who would control the regions inhabited by Arabs, Turkmens, and Kurds in the future began in the area held by the rebels and the IS.

The YPG/YPJ offensive against the rebels in A'zaz was probably primarily the result of the assessment that a government army breakthrough to A'zaz would make establishing a connection between the Kurdish cantons impossible, and therefore any further advance of the government had to be prevented. On February 15, 2016, the YPG/YPJ captured the town of Tal Rifaat (south of A'zaz) with its twenty thousand inhabitants and proceeded to occupy the southern part of the remaining rebel enclave around A'zaz, without, however, taking the city itself. The Kurdish advance against Turkish allies led to the intervention of the Turkish army. On February 19, Turkish artillery fire from Kilis and Sucuköy to the west of Afrin hit the city center, killing two civilians. In addition, the villages of Deir Ballout, Hamam, Kafr Janneh, Meşalê Hêgicê, Senarê, Anqelê, Firîrê, Hec Hesnê, and Avraz came under fire, killing three members of a family. The Turkish army advanced about three hundred meters [nine hundred feet] into Syrian territory and destroyed about five hundred olive trees in order to close its three-meter-high [nine feet] concrete wall at the Syrian border.[5]

In the end, the race for the corridor between Afrin and Kobanê was won not by the SDF but by Turkey. The most important turning point was the conquest by Turkish troops and militias of al-Bab, on February 23, 2017.

When the Syrian government army conquered Tadef on February 26, 2017, it was confronted with pro-Turkish rebels—this meant that the SDF would have had to enter into military conflict with either the Syrian army or the Turkish troops and its allies, something that the Kurds chose to avoid. But as YPG speaker Rêdûr Xelîl told me in an interview, the reasons for relinquishing the corridor were actually political and not military.[6] The precise background of these decisions remains a matter of speculation to this day. But it seems very likely that the U.S., as the most important ally of the SDF, imposed a veto on any additional advance to avoid further provoking its NATO ally Turkey.

---

5   Ibid., 143.
6   Interview with Rêdûr Xelîl, February 14, 2017.

Russia's Role in Afrin

But even so, the SDF did not thereby become a mere extension of the U.S., since it also tried to hedge its bets vis-à-vis Russia, not least because in 2017 there were increasing signs of an impending division of Syria into a Russian and a U.S. sphere of influence with a border running along the Euphrates, thus placing Afrin in the Russian sphere.

The PYD had unofficial representatives in Moscow from the beginning of the Syrian civil war. In October 2015, the Russian ambassador in Ankara, Andrey Karlow, had explained to the Russian news agency Ria Novosti that his country did not regard either the PKK or the PYD as terrorist organizations.[7] With these words, ambassador Karlow, who later, under circumstances that remain unclear to this day, was shot to death by a Turkish policeman during a speech at the opening of a photo exhibition in Ankara on December 19, 2016,[8] made clear that Russia, unlike the Western negotiators in Geneva, perceived the PYD as a partner in future peace talks about Syria, while at the same time distancing himself from the Turkish position that the PKK, the PYD, and the YPG were terrorist organizations.

In February 2016, the PYD opened an official liaison office for West Kurdistan in Moscow that functioned as a kind of unofficial embassy. Finally, on March 19, 2016, an agreement was reached that led to the establishment of a field office of the so-called Russian Reconciliation Center directly at the front line between the SDF and the pro-Turkish militias.[9] This "Reconciliation Center" began operating on February 23, 2016 and had its main seat in the Russian Khmeimim Air Base, near Latakia. It primarily monitored ceasefires between Syrian government troops and various militias. It also coordinated aid deliveries to areas under government control or under the control of militias that had concluded ceasefire

---

7   "Syria's Kurds to Open First European Office in Moscow," *Rûdaw*, February 7, 2016, accessed September 30, 2018, http://www.rudaw.net/english/middleeast/syria/070220161.

8   "Mevlut Mert Altintas: Turkish Policeman Who Shot Russia's Envoy," *BBC News*, December 20, 2016, accessed September 30, 2018, https://www.bbc.com/news/world-europe-38377419.

9   Thomas Schmidinger, "Militärische Expansion mit US-Unterstützung: Aktuelle Entwicklungen in Syrisch-Kurdistan," in *Wiener Jahrbuch für Kurdische Studien 5: Sprache—Migration—Zusammenhalt: Kurdisch und seine Diaspora*, ed. Katharina Brizić et al. (Vienna: Praesens Verlag, 2017), 237.

agreements with the government. The field office in Afrin, however, was mainly tasked with monitoring the ceasefire between pro-Turkish militias and the SDF.

At first, the Kurds in Afrin regarded the Russian presence as a security guarantee against Turkish invasion. However, in the summer of 2017, when it became increasingly clear that there were secret agreements between Russia and the U.S. concerning the division of Syria into separate spheres of influence and that Afrin would be a part of the Russian sphere, the Reconciliation Center field office became the most important point of contact with the Russian military in Syria.

The increasingly close contact with the U.S. was likely the more important development for the Democratic Federation of Northern Syria's general project. Simultaneously, the growing military and political dependency of the SDF on the U.S. in Kobanê and the Cizîrê led to an increasingly problematic relationship with Russia and, thus, to a mounting marginalization of Afrin. In the end, the SDF was not invited to the negotiations in Astana and publicly declared that they did not intend to abide by the results.[10]

---

10 "U.S-Backed Syrian SDF Forces Refuse to Support Astana Meeting Results," *Ekurd Daily*, January 19, 2017, accessed September 30, 2018, http://www.kurdishinstitute.be/u-s-backed-syrian-sdf-forces-refuse-to-support-astana-meeting-results/.

Kurdish Enclaves in the Afrin Area

The fact that the key regions of Afrin had long been almost exclusively inhabited by Kurds does not mean that there were clearly demarcated settlement areas for the various ethnic groups in northwestern Syria. Until 2018, East of Afrin, between the town of A'zaz and the Kurdish areas of Kobanê, there was a linguistically mixed area, with Arab, Kurdish, and Turkmen villages and small towns. In Manbij (Kurdish: Minbic), which was captured by the YPG and its allies in 2016, apart from an Arab majority and Turkmen and Kurdish minorities, there were also a number of Chechens and Circassians. Most of the Kurdish villages were located in the middle, between the predominantly Arab cities of A'zaz and Jarābulus. Some of Kurdish population of this area had fled from their villages when the Islamic State took over the region around Jarābulus in 2013. Until 2015, the villages farther to the west were still to some degree under the protection of the Jabhat al-Akrad (Kurdish: Enîya Kurdan), which retained a certain presence there among the opposition groups. After 2015, this became increasingly impossible. In part, other pro-Turkish Kurdish militias assumed responsibility for the protection of these Kurdish villages, among them the Descendants of Saladin Brigade (Liwa aḥfād Ṣalāḥ ad-Dīn), led by Mahmūd Khalo, and the Azadî Battalion, which had been founded by members of Mustafa Cumaa's Azadî Party but whose bond with the political party seems to have withered in the period following the party's 2014 merger with three other parties to form the Democratic Party of Kurdistan-Syria (PDKS), the sister party of Barzani's Democratic Party of Kurdistan-Iraq. Although Cumaa emulated the PDKS on his Facebook page, condemning the Turkish attack on Afrin as "Turkish terrorism,"

The city of Afrin grew considerably once the civil war began, with widespread construction to accommodate Kurds from Aleppo and other contested towns.

the Azadî Battalion, under his commander Azad Shabo, participated in this attack.

Between A'zaz and the canton of Afrin there was once a small Êzîdî village, Elî Qîno. Elî Qîno was located west of the wall that the YPG/YPJ had erected at the border of the area under its control and was thus effectively controlled by pro-Turkish rebels. On Monday, June 12, 2017, the Êzîdî population of the village were obliged to leave their homes with only one hour's notice. The inhabitants fled to Afrin, and their houses were confiscated by pro-Turkish rebels.[1]

South of Afrin, there were yet other Kurdish settlements in enclaves in linguistically mixed regions, where, apart from Kurdish, Arabic and Turkmen were spoken. Thus, the small town of Til Eren (Arabic: Tal Aran), with 17,700 inhabitants, and the nearby town of Tal Hasil/Tal Hasel about ten kilometers [six miles] southeast of Aleppo were predominantly

---

1   Thomas Schmidinger, "Militärische Expansion mit US-Unterstützung: Aktuelle Entwicklungen in Syrisch-Kurdistan," in *Wiener Jahrbuch für Kurdische Studien 5: Sprache—Migration—Zusammenhalt: Kurdisch und seine Diaspora*, ed. Katharina Brizić et al. (Vienna: Praesens Verlag, 2017), 329.

Kurdish. During the civil war, these Kurdish enclaves were conquered by fighters from the Islamic State in Iraq and Sham (ISIS) and other Islamist opposition groups, on August 1, 2013.[2] While they held them, the control over these two locations was at least in part exercised by the Azadî Battalion, under Azad Shabo, but in November 2013, they were recaptured by the Syrian government army and have since been firmly held by the Syrian regime.

There is also a Kurdish district in Aleppo that proclaimed itself autonomous when fighting began in the town and positioned itself as a kind of neutral zone between the areas respectively ruled by the regime and the opposition. At first, the Kurdish People's Protection Units assumed control of both the Sheikh Masqood (Kurdish: Şêxmeqsûd) district in the north of the city and adjacent district of Ashrafiya, which is closer to the city center. Like the Kurdish areas in northern Syria, the two districts fell to the Kurds without a fight, because the regime needed its forces for its struggle against the opposition and the Kurds guaranteed them a peaceful withdrawal. But the neutrality of the district was difficult to sustain, and the PYD's control remained precarious. After the split of the Free Syrian Army (FSA) in September 2013 and the intra-oppositional civil war between secular forces and the Islamic coalition, which eventually morphed into the Islamic Front (al-Jabhat al-Islāmiyyah) in November 2013, the relationship between the Kurds and the opposition steadily worsened. Following the victory of the Islamic Front over the FSA's secular brigades, the part of Aleppo ruled by the opposition was also taken over by groups including the jihadist Ahrar ash-Sham, the Liwa al-Tawhid, and the Harakat Nur ad-Din az-Zanki. These groups were all seeking to establish an Islamic state in Syria but were hostile to the secular opposition and to the so-called Islamic State and Jabhat al-Nusra, the Syrian al-Qaeda affiliate. While the Kurdish YPG had begun to coordinate its actions with the secular former FSA brigades expelled by the Islamic Front in 2014,

---

2   In 2013, what was later to become the IS was still calling itself Islamic State in Iraq and Sham (Greater Syria), which in Europe was abbreviated as ISIS. At the time, there continued to be instances of cooperation between ISIS and other Islamist opposition groups. It was only with the establishment of a state-like entity in early 2014 and the attempt to eliminate all other groups that such ventures became impossible. Since 2014, ISIS (or, since the summer of 2014, the IS) has been in strict opposition to all other groups, including other jihadist organizations.

Refugees from Aleppo wait at the Afrin city park for work as day laborers.

finally joining them to form the Syrian Democratic Forces (SDF) in 2015, the relationship between the Turkish-backed Islamist opposition and the YPG worsened. In Aleppo, there were attacks on the Kurdish districts not just by Ahrar ash-Sham, the Liwa al-Tawhid, and the Harakat Nur ad-Din az-Zanki but also by the regime. In the end, in 2014, Ashrafiya was gradually handed over to the regime piecemeal, while Şêxmeqsûd was retained as a Kurdish refuge in Aleppo.

The attacks by the Islamist opposition brigades finally contributed to a state of affairs in which the Kurdish units in Aleppo, even though they did not actively participate in the conquest of East Aleppo, then still under opposition control, at least partially cooperated and coordinated with the regime, a course that for a time allowed the district to survive, even after the withdrawal of the opposition in December 2016. In the end, Şêxmeqsûd was not captured by the government army but was handed over to the regime incrementally. In the face of an economic blockade by the regime, a partial return of the latter was negotiated in December 2017, accompanied by the hoisting of the Syrian flag. But the YPG remained present until February 22, 2018. It was only the Turkish attack on Afrin that finally led to the withdrawal of the Kurdish forces from Aleppo. A statement by the YPG/YPJ says that in the face of the silence of the world powers about the barbaric attacks of the Turkish state, all YPG and YPJ forces had to be withdrawn from Aleppo and redirected to Afrin, and that this was the reason why the Kurdish neighborhoods in Aleppo had once again come under the control of regime forces.[3]

3   "YPG Statement on Aleppo," *ANF News*, February 22, 2018, accessed September 30, 2018, https://anfenglish.com/features/ypg-statement-on-aleppo-25083.

The War against Afrin

The war Turkey waged against Afrin beginning in January 2018 didn't just destroy Kurdish autonomy, it threatens to undermine Kurdish existence at the "Mountain of the Kurds" as a whole. A book cannot be produced as quickly as newspapers or websites and can thus never be totally up-to-date. The war that is being waged against Afrin while this book is being produced will presumably still be ongoing when it appears, will have cost hundreds of additional civilian lives, and will continue the expulsion of the Kurdish population.

Long before the actual war, the Turkish government in Ankara, first and foremost President Erdoğan, openly called for war against the Kurds in Syria, particularly in Afrin. One reason for this was Turkey's fear of having a territory at its southern border ruled by a sister party of its enemy the PKK. There are also clear domestic reasons. Recep Tayyip Erdoğan is a weak president whose increasingly authoritarian policies since 2016 have gained him numerous domestic opponents.

However, just as in many states worldwide, in Turkey, when the country is at war, the political actors rally behind their "commander in chief" (Turkish: Başkomutan), as Erdoğan has been called in Turkish newspapers and in publications by institutions close to the AKP in Europe since the beginning of the war. In Turkey, all of the important political forces now stand behind the "commander in chief," among them the hitherto strongest opposition party, the Kemalist Republican People's Party (CHP), and the Good Party (Turkish: İyi Parti), led by Meral Akşener, which only split from the right-wing extremist Nationalist Movement Party (MHP) in October 2017 because of the latter's overly pro-AKP positions.

Apart from the pro-Kurdish left, the People's Democratic Party (HDP), which has been severely weakened by many arrests, there isn't a single parliamentary party that hasn't unequivocally rallied behind the war and its "Başkomutan." from that point of view, Erdoğan's calculations seem to have worked out, at least domestically.

In all of this, Turkey's goal is not just to conquer Afrin and to expel the YPG/YPJ but also to ethnically cleanse the entire region. At a rally in Bursa on January 21, 2018, the day after the start of the war, President Erdoğan proclaimed, contrary to all facts, that 55 percent of the population were Arab and only 35 percent were Kurds, while the rest were Turkmens, and that he was planning to return the area to its "rightful owners."[1] Given the fact that the actual percentage of the Kurdish population in Afrin was far greater than 90 percent, this proclamation can only be interpreted as the announcement of ethnic cleansing to achieve an Arabization and Turkmenization of the region. And, in reality, the first steps in that direction were undertaken in March by moving Arab and Turkmen settlers into evacuated villages and towns.

Turkish War Preparations

By the summer of 2017, it was clear that Turkey intended to proceed militarily against Afrin. President Erdoğan and the members of his government made increasingly open threats against Afrin but apparently still hesitated, because they had not received the green light from Russia for a military intervention. On the other hand, the lack of international reaction against the open threats of war and the persistent close cooperation of the EU around the refugee questions certainly contributed to Turkey's continuing pursuit of its attack plans.

For international public consumption, the Turkish side continued to claim that the YPG posed a "terrorist" threat, even though there hadn't been a single documented attack by the YPG on Turkish territory, at most responses to Turkish cross-border artillery attacks: the Turkish government was unable to prove a single YPG attack on Turkish territory or to put forth any credible evidence of plans for such attacks.

---

1   "Erdogan Says Afrin Is Majority Arab, Threatens Arabization," *Kurdistan 24*, January 21, 2018, accessed September 30, 2018, http://www.kurdistan24.net/en/news/7899b6c9-f475-40fb-a9bc-ffda4b69f0df.

Even such a sharp critic of the PKK and the PYD as the Berlin Kurdologist Eva Savelsberg, who cooperates closely with the Kurdish National Council (ENKS) and the pro-Turkish wing of the Syrian opposition, concedes that the Turkish attack on Afrin was "undoubtedly an illegitimate violation of international law." In a March 15, 2018, interview otherwise very critical of the PKK and the PYD, she explained: "Turkey now claims it was attacked from there, but to the best of my knowledge it has never documented the claim. Missiles were fired only after Turkey had already begun its offensive."[2]

That there was no threat to Turkey emanating from Afrin is also documented by the fact that the guerilla activities of the PKK in Turkey did not take place in the vicinity of Afrin but hundreds of kilometers [hundreds of miles] to the east, for the most part in the mountainous border region adjacent to Iraq—nowhere near Kilis, Gaziantep, or Hatay.

It seems that at the outset Turkey hoped its Kurdish allies in the region would spearhead the attack on Afrin. However, the most important pro-Turkish Kurdish militia in the region, Mahmūd Khalo's six-hundred-man Descendants of Saladin Brigade, opposed the plan and by July 2017 had rejected participating in a pro-Turkish attack on Afrin. Turkey's reaction was simply to dissolve the brigade, which had been founded in 2015. The commander of the brigade was arrested by pro-Turkish Arab militias and, he claims, tortured.[3] A small remnant of the brigade was reactivated by Turkey in autumn 2017 to create at least a semblance of Kurdish participation in the attack on Afrin. The real size of the new Descendants of Saladin Brigade is hard to estimate, but it probably does not count more than one hundred fighters.

As discussed above, it appears that by the summer of 2017, Russia and the U.S. had agreed on a division of Syria into spheres of influence. Though the agreement remained secret, and the details will probably only be made public at some point in the future, many observers of Syria now

---

2   "Das Personal der PKK und der YPG ist dasselbe," *T-online*, March 15, 2018, accessed October 1, 2018, http://www.t-online.de/nachrichten/ausland/krisen/id_83390548/kurdologin-zu-afrin-und-den-folgen-das-personal-der-pkk-und-der-ypg-ist-dasselbe-.html.

3   Thomas Schmidinger, "Militärische Expansion mit US-Unterstützung: Aktuelle Entwicklungen in Syrisch-Kurdistan," in *Wiener Jahrbuch für Kurdische Studien 5: Sprache—Migration—Zusammenhalt: Kurdisch und seine Diaspora*, ed. Katharina Brizić et al. (Vienna: Praesens Verlag, 2017), 239.

assume that Russia and the U.S. must have agreed on the Euphrates as the demarcation line of their respective spheres of influence at some point in early 2017. The U.S. persisted in its military support of the SDF in the northeast of Syria and, in January 2018, even announced the founding of a professionally trained border protection unit consisting of thirty thousand fighters drafted from members of the SDF, an announcement that angered Ankara and infuriated Moscow.[4] At the same time, the U.S. repeatedly made it clear that it didn't regard itself as responsible for Afrin or the Kurdish district of Aleppo.

Throughout the autumn, intense diplomatic activity took place between Russia and Turkey. In November and December 2017, Putin and Erdoğan met three times within a month. Of course, we do not have any concrete information about the agreements that were reached in these private talks, but we can clearly see that Turkey coordinated with Russia before the attack on Afrin, and that Putin and Erdoğan had clearly arrived at some sort of agreement about the future of Syria, with Afrin one of the victims of the agreement.

On January 23, three days after the start of the war, the Russian government news channel RT, which has the character of a semiofficial Russian government media organ, commented that "the Astana protecting powers," that is, Russia and Turkey, had "entered into a non-public agreement in which Ankara commits itself to cease its support for the Islamist organization Hayat Tahrir al-Sham and the latter's allies in Idlib and to no longer regard the operations of the Syrian army east of Idlib and in the direction of the town itself as a violation of the de-escalation agreements that had been reached in Sochi the previous year. On the other hand, Russia has withdrawn its contingent from Afrin and will not intervene against the Turkish army's operation 'Olive Branch.'"[5]

With this, the "non-public" horse trade between Russia and Turkey is publicly acknowledged. It is, however, doubtful that the deal was only about the Hayat Tahrir al-Sham in Idlib, the largest area in Syria still held by Arab rebels.

---

4   "U.S.-Backed Force Could Cement a Kurdish Enclave in Syria," *New York Times*, January 16, 2018, accessed October 1, 2018, https://www.nytimes.com/2018/01/16/world/middleeast/syria-kurds-force.html.

5   "Analyse: Wieso Russland die Türkei bei ihrer Offensive in Afrin gewähren lässt," *RT Deutsch*, January 23, 2018, accessed October 1, 2018, https://deutsch.rt.com/meinung/64015-wieso-russland-turkei-afrin-offensive/.

The timing of the massive attacks by the Syrian regime on the eastern suburbs of Damascus still held by various oppositional militias, particularly, on East Ghouta,[6] seems to indicate that this bartering between Turkey and Russia also involved other areas. The Turkish-Russian deal was quite likely struck on the backs of the Kurds in Afrin and the civilians in East Ghouta: Turkey would cease its support for the rebels and not oppose the conquest of East Ghouta, and Russia would give Turkey a free hand in Afrin.

Moreover, it is certainly possible that the Turkish-Russian secret agreement includes other rebel enclaves in Central Syria that the regime could attack after the reconquest of East Ghouta. At any rate, there is a lot evidence indicating that the regime's current objective is to destroy the rebel enclaves in the key Syrian areas in order to fortify its own position in any postwar order. The rebel enclaves north of Homs, in particular, as well as those to the northeast of Damascus, between al-Naseriyah and al-Dumayr, still represent an obstacle to the regime's comprehensive control of the central area. To carry out its project undisturbed, it was perhaps necessary to appease the most important supporter of various rebel groups, namely, Turkey. If so, the suffering of the civilians in Afrin and East Ghouta would obviously be a consequence of the arrangement between Ankara and Moscow.

But for Moscow and its ally, the Syrian regime, the attacks by Tukey had a second positive effect. They served to punish the YPG/YPJ for cooperating with the U.S., and, simultaneously, to push it into the arms of the regime. In December 2017, the Syrian flag was again hoisted in the Kurdish district of Aleppo, Şêxmeqsûd, which has been under the control of the YPG since 2012, without the district being conquered by the Syrian army. Actually, the partial reintegration of the district, with its approximately thirty thousand inhabitants, represented a basic precondition for the cessation of the blockade of the area. The end of 2017 saw the resumption of the delivery of fuel and food to Şêxmeqsûd. Such a piecemeal reintegration into the regime's hands might represent one possible YPG/YPJ reaction to

---

6   "Ghouta" is the name for the irrigation oasis that includes the Syrian capital of Damascus. The eastern region fell into the hands of oppositionists in 2011, but they were encircled by 2012, and then dissolved into various militias that were in part in conflict with each other and included, alongside moderate rebel groups, the Hayat Tahrir al-Sham (the successor organization to the al-Qaeda militia Jabhat al-Nusra) and another jihadist organization, Ahrar ash-Sham.

YPJ fighters participated in the resistance to the 2018 Turkish invasion.

the Turkish attack. In September 2017, Russian media had speculated that a comparable step could also be undertaken in Afrin. On January 22, Alder Khalil, a leading member of the Movement for a Democratic Society (TEV-DEM), the PYD's mass organization, stated that Russia had openly exerted pressure on the administration in Afrin to relinquish the region to the regime and let the latter defend Afrin against Turkey. He claims that the Kurdish side rejected this "offer."[7]

But even if such a ploy fails, for Russia this is a win-win situation. Should the YPG/YPJ not submit itself to the control of the regime, by cooperating with Turkey, Russia could at least drive a wedge between NATO and Ankara and possibly bind the latter strategically to Moscow instead of the West, which is not much loved by the Turkish leadership, as it is. Russia would thereby profit from the Turkish attack however it unfolds.

In Turkey, the attack on Afrin was extensively prepared for with propaganda. Any failure to support the war was treated as treason, and critics were intimidated and even legally prosecuted. The nonreaction to the Turkish announcement of war in Europe and the clear positioning of the U.S., which stated that it was not responsible for the Kurds west of the Euphrates, certainly also encouraged the regime in Ankara to actually carry out its war designs.

The Beginning of the War

On January 20, 2018, the Turkish army finally began with its offensive against Afrin, which it cynically chose to call "Operation Olive Branch" (Turkish: Zeytin Dalı Harekâtı). Contrary to all facts, Turkish prime minister Binali Yıldırım told the media that the Turkish offensive was directed against all "terrorists," that is, the YPG and the IS, and that these two groups were fighting "side by side."[8]

The impudence of this propaganda lie by the Turkish prime minister is demonstrated by the fact that the YPG has been the IS's main enemy in Syria and had borne the brunt of the struggle against this force. Moreover,

---

7   Thomas Schmidinger, "Türkische Truppen in Syrien: Ausweitung der Kampfzone," *derStandard.at*, January 22, 2018, accessed October 1, 2018, https://derstandard.at/2000072706997/Tuerkische-Truppen-in-Syrien-Ausweitung-der-Kampfzone?_blogGroup=1.

8   "IŞİD ile YPG omuz omuza savaşıyor," *Timeturk*, January 22, 2018, accessed October 1, 2018, https://www.timeturk.com/isid-ile-ypg-omuz-omuza-savasiyor/haber-833707.

and not least because of the military successes of the YPG/YPJ against the IS in 2016, there were no IS fighters anywhere near Afrin by this point. At the beginning of 2018, there were only remnants of IS territory. Nevertheless, the Turkish government still tried to convince the international public that its battle targeted both the IS and the YPG.

In order to be able to advance into Syrian territory parts of the three-meter-high [nine feet] concrete wall that Turkey had erected at the Syrian border over the previous years had to be dismantled, so that the militiamen and soldiers could cross the border with their tanks.

In Turkey, the start of the war was celebrated with a wave of religiously charged propaganda of the first order. On the first day of the fighting, under orders from the Turkish Presidium for Religious Affairs (Turkish: Diyanet İşleri Başkanlığı), Turkish mosques practically called for a jihad by reciting surah 48 (al-Fatah, or "victory"). This was not just the case at mosques in Turkey, the same was true for the umbrella organizations in Europe supported by the Presidium for Religious Affairs: simultaneously with the mosques in the motherland, this prayer for the victory of the Turkish army was recited in the mosques of the registered association, the Turkish-Islamic Union of the Institution for Religion (DİTİB) in Germany and its Austrian counterpart, the Turkish-Islamic Union for Cultural and Social Cooperation (Turkish: Avusturya Türkiye İslam Birliği, ATİB). Since then, regular prayers for the Turkish soldiers and their victory have taken place in many of these semi-official Turkish mosques in Europe.

Since the start of the war, the Turkish media have referred to Erdoğan all but exclusively as the "commander in chief." Anyone who dares to publicly criticize the war faces the possibility of arrest and trial for "terrorist propaganda." Even though almost all the critical dailies in Turkey have been banned in recent years and more than one hundred journalists had been jailed even before the war,[9] since the start of the war more journalists, politicians (mainly from the HDP), and activists have been arrested. One hundred and fifty critics of the attack on Afrin were jailed in the four

---

9   Susanne Güsten, "Türkei: Hoffnung für mehr als 100 Journalisten in Haft," *Die Presse*, January 11, 2018, accessed October 1, 2018, https://diepresse.com/home/ausland/welt/5352072/Tuerkei_Hoffnung-fuer-mehr-als-100-Journalisten-in-Haft.

days from January 20 to January 24. Some of them were released after a few hours, while others were held.[10]

"Commander in chief" Erdoğan himself frequently describes his critics as "terrorist lovers" during his public appearances. Even the largest umbrella organization of Turkish doctors, the Turkish Doctors' Association (Turkish: Türk Tabipleri Birliği, TTB) is now among the groups that have suffered repression since the beginning of the war. At the end of January, after criticizing the attack on Afrin, eleven leading members of this organization, which counts about 80 percent of all doctors in Turkey among its members, were arrested for "propaganda for a terrorist organization" and "incitement of the people to hatred and hostility."[11] Because they warned of the humanitarian consequences of the attack, Erdoğan berated the officials of the Doctors' Association as "agents of imperialism," "scum," and, as mentioned, "terrorist lovers."

In reality, the Turkish army was only in the second row of the fighting in the war against Afrin. The war's foot soldiers were the Syrian militias marching side by side with, or, rather, in front of, the Turkish soldiers. These allies represented a very heterogeneous mix of militiamen. Turkey's references to them as the "Free Syrian Army" can safely be described as mere propaganda. As already noted above, the Free Syrian Army actually ceased to exist in northern Syria in autumn 2013. Individual groups continue to use this label, particularly in the south of the country, but since the secular brigades split and were dislodged in autumn 2013, the previous loose joint structure of armed resistance in Syria that existed between 2011 and 2013 is no more and any remnants are by no means identical with it.

The fighters on the Turkish side represent a mixture of soldiers, desperados, and Islamists. Some of them probably chose to participate because they saw an opportunity for themselves and their families. On March 13, a ranking commander of the pro-Turkish militias claimed that

---

10 Sybille Klormann et al., "Zehra, Ayşenur, Mehmet—angeklagt wegen Journalismus," *Zeit Online*, March 13, 2017, accessed October 1, 2018, http://www.zeit.de/gesellschaft/zeitgeschehen/2017-03/pressefreiheit-tuerkei-inhaftierte-journalisten-deniz-yuecel-freedeniz.

11 "Türkei führt bei Ärzten durch, die Militäreinsatz kritisieren," *derStandard.at*, January 30, 2018, accessed October 1, 2018, https://derstandard.at/2000073289605/Tuerkische-fuehrt-Razzien-bei-Aerzten-durch-die-Militaereinsatz-kritisierten.

the Turkish government guaranteed its Syrian allies that the families of fallen soldiers would be awarded Turkish citizenship.[12] But there were also politically motivated people among the pro-Turkish allies with a long history of conflict with the Syrian Kurds who saw the opportunity to take revenge for the defeat of the IS: jihadists who were by this point fighting their enemies alongside Turkey.

Jihadist Fighters in Afrin

Since the beginning of the attacks by Turkey and its Syrian allies on Afrin, the Kurdish side made the claim that Turkey was fighting the YPG alongside jihadist fighters. At the same time, Turkey claimed to be fighting not just the YPG but also the IS. As noted above, the latter claim is easily exposed as a propaganda lie, since by January 2018 there hadn't been any IS fighters in the vicinity of Afrin for at least two years. In 2018, the last remnants of the areas controlled by the IS were located at the Syrian-Iraqi border north of the Euphrates, reaching from the small town of Hajin to Syria's border with Iraq. In addition, there were a few steppe areas further to the north, as well as at the southern edge of the Golan, in the area bordering Jordan, where the IS-allied Khalid ibn al-Walid army controlled a few villages. On the other hand, surviving IS fighters had fled to Turkey in late 2017 after being defeated in Syria. It would not be very surprising if some of these fighters had joined other militias in order to make their way back into Syria. It is hard to assess what proportion of the Turkish allies is made up of former IS fighters, but there is clear evidence that the YPG's claims that IS fighters are involved in the attack on Afrin is accurate.

A former IS fighter who was still in close contact with his former companions told the British paper the *Independent* (February 7, 2018): "Most of those who are fighting in Afrin against the YPG are Isis, though Turkey has trained them to change their assault tactics." According to him, Turkey deceived the public by claiming to fight the Islamic State, while in reality, it trained the IS fighters. Similarly, at least one known IS fighter from Vienna was killed in Afrin in February 2018 in the battle against the YPG. The European jihadists regard the fighters of the YPG

---

12 "Turkish Government Grants Citizenship for Families of FSA Members Killed in Syria's Afrin," *SOL International*, March 13, 2018, accessed October 1, 2018, http://news.sol.org.tr/turkish-government-grants-citizenship-families-fsa-members-killed-syrias-afrin-174283.

An ambulance from Germany flies the YPG flag.

and the YPJ as *mushrikūn*, that is, as idolaters and polytheists. This is also the term that they use for the two armies. A former IS fighter from Austria told the author of this book that he knew at least some former fellow fighters who were fighting against the YPG in Afrin. In addition, there have been increasingly numerous videos by fighters in the pro-Turkish militias speaking out against Kurds with unequivocally jihadist rhetoric—and more and more reports of decapitations of Kurdish fighters. But how systematic the recruitment of former IS fighters and other adherents of various currents of political Islam (including jihadists) by the Turkish army and its allies really was cannot be safely assessed on the basis of these statements alone.

The really problematic factor here, however, was that even groups that hadn't fought with the IS before but hailed from other political Islamist militias increasingly resorted to a similar rhetoric, with even seemingly moderate Islamists legitimizing severe war crimes. At the end of February 2018, the Syrian Islamic Council, an umbrella organization of oppositional non-jihadist religious scholars that has been characterized as "moderate[ly] Islamic" by the Carnegie Middle East Center,[13] announced

---

13   Thomas Pierret, "The Syrian Islamic Council," March 13, 2014, *Carnegie Middle East Center*, accessed October 1, 2018, http://carnegie-mec.org/diwan/55580.

a fatwa according to which the battle against the YPG and the SDF was a jihad and captured fighters could be executed. Even though the fatwa signed by ten Islamic scholars stated that noncombatants, that is, women, children, and old people, were not to be killed but to be treated respectfully, with regard to any enemy fighters captured in the war, it explained that the "mujahedin" were free "to do with them whatever they please."[14] Fighters in the pro-Turkish militias fully understood what this meant: it was a free pass to murder, torture, and rape prisoners of war.

Reactions to the Attack

The international reaction to the attack was muted. The EU, Russia, and the U.S. all failed to firmly condemn the attack. The EU, for example, didn't suspend a single one of its programs in Turkey. As noted above, Germany even approved additional permits for the delivery of war materiel. The sharpest condemnation of the attack came from a relatively powerless body, the European Parliament. On March 15, a large majority at the parliament called on Turkey to end its military intervention, asking the Turkish government to withdraw its troops and to make "a constructive contribution."[15]

The Turkish president Erdoğan reacted angrily and was quoted by the pro-government Turkish media as having said, "Hey, European Parliament, keep your admonitions to yourself."[16] Erdoğan was apparently well aware that he had nothing to fear from the European Parliament as long as the most important European governments continued to support him. After all, in the intergovernmental construction of Europe the locus of political power continues to reside with either the Council or the governments of the EU member states and not with the democratically elected European Parliament. That there was no need for the Turkish regime to be afraid of the powerful states of Europe was demonstrated to the Turkish foreign minister Mevlüt Çavuşoğlu as recently as March 2018, during

---

14 "Fatwa no. 11 of the Syrian National Council," accessed October 1, 2018, http://sy-sic.com/?p=6465.

15 "EU-Parlament verlangt Ende der Angriffe auf Afrin," *Zeit Online*, March 15, 2018, accessed October 1, 2018, http://www.zeit.de/politik/ausland/2018-03/kurdenmiliz-ypg-syrien-afrin-krieg-tuerkei-eu-parlament.

16 "Erdogan zu EU: 'Behalte deine Belehrung für dich!'" *TurkishPress*, March 16, 2018, accessed October 1, 2018, https://turkishpress.de/news/politik/16-03-2018/erdogan-zu-eu-behalte-deine-belehrung-fuer-dich.

THE WAR AGAINST AFRIN

his visit in Germany. Instead of having to deal with criticism about the war in Afrin, Çavuşoğlu brashly demanded that Germany arrest the PYD politician Salih Muslim.[17] The then foreign minister of Germany Sigmar Gabriel (SPD) refrained from criticizing the war in Afrin in any meaningful way. On the contrary, Çavuşoğlu had hardly even left Germany for Austria when the Kurdish publisher Mezopotamien Verlag in Neuss was raided and had four truckloads of books and other items seized.[18]

During his official visit to Austria, Çavuşoğlu was also carefully shielded from demonstrators and any criticism of the attack on Afrin. After the meeting, the daily *Kurier* reported that the Austrian foreign minister Karin Kneissl (FPÖ) "received and courted her Turkish ministerial colleague."[19]

At the same time, Russia and Turkey announced increased military cooperation. On the same day that the European Parliament reprimanded Erdoğan for the war against Afrin, the Russian foreign minister Sergey Lavrov responded to a Turkish query by announcing that Russia intended to accelerate the delivery of Russian S-400 air defense systems to Turkey.[20] This may merely have been a Turkish attempt to send a warning signal to its NATO partners, but it might also have been the first sign of an end to NATO as we know it. When criticized, Turkey has repeatedly threatened to turn its back on the West and to side with Russia. Nobody knows how serious this is this time, how the U.S. will react to it, or what the consequences will be for the relationship between the SDF and the U.S. in the region. Even now, Erdoğan is threatening to next attack the Kurdish areas east of the Euphrates, in the U.S. sphere of influence. At the same time, there have been negotiations with the government in Baghdad about a

---

17 "Turkey Asks Germany to Arrest and Extradite Former PYD Co-Chair Salih Muslim," *Hürriyet Daily News*, March 5, 2018, accessed November 3, 2018, http://www.hurriyetdailynews.com/turkey-demands-ypg-former-chairs-temporary-arrest-from-germany-128245.

18 "German Police Confiscate Thousands of Books and CDs," *ANF News*, March 11, 2018, accessed October 1, 2018, https://anfenglishmobile.com/news/german-police-confiscate-thousands-of-books-and-cds-25406.

19 "Österreich-Türkei: Lipizzaner und Trippelschritte," *Kurier.at*, March 8, 2018, accessed October 1, 2018, https://kurier.at/politik/ausland/kneissl-empfing-cavusoglu/313.255.670.

20 "Russia to Speed Up S-400 Deliveries to Turkey—Lavrov," *RT*, March 15, 2018, accessed October 1, 2018, https://www.rt.com/news/421335-turkey-s400-complex-deliveries/.

This baker demonstrates his allegiance to rival Kurdish movements by hanging a poster with the portraits of Kurdish leaders as diverse as Abdullah Öcalan, Jalal Talabani, and Masoud and Mullah Mustafa Barzani.

large-scale attack on PKK areas in Iraq. Here the risk of acting against U.S. interests is far greater than is the case with the attack on Afrin.

The War in Afrin and the Kurdish Opposition

The opponents of Kurdish autonomy, be it in Iraq or Syria, can also always rely on internal Kurdish conflicts, which they can instrumentalize. The lack of democracy and the nonexistent broader cooperation of the Kurdish parties were certainly not the reason for the Turkish attack. But in this case the internal Kurdish conflicts have made it easier for Turkey to enforce its own interests. The long history of conflicts between the ruling PYD in Afrin and its allies, on the one hand, and with the ENKS, on the other hand, only played a minor role in this war, but the war is being further complicated by yet another conflict.

This is so despite the fact that the main rival of the ruling PYD, the ENKS, condemned the Turkish attack as early as January 22, 2018.[21] Some of the ENKS supporters even felt prompted to move closer to the PYD in response to Turkey's attack, particularly those who had family ties with

---

21 *Yekîtî Media*, accessed October 1, 2018, https://ara.yekiti-media.org.

Afrin. But much to the disappointment of many Kurds, the ENKS has not withdrawn from the National Coalition of the Syrian Revolutionary and Oppositional Forces, even though this body is dominated by pro-Turkish oppositionists and openly supported the war against Afrin. This not only led to criticism on the part of political forces close to the PYD but was also denounced by the Society for Threatened Peoples (Gesellschaft für bedrohte Völker, GfbV) in Germany, among others. In a press release sent out on February 5, 2018, the society's spokesperson for the Middle East, Kamal Sido, who is himself from Afrin (albeit not a sympathizer of the PYD, but rather a liberal and a member of the German Free Democratic Party, FDP), criticized the German support for this alliance: "We know that, for example, the National Coalition of the Syrian Revolutionary and Oppositional Forces maintains a liaison office in Berlin and that repre-sentatives of this movement appear at various events. On its website, this National Coalition openly makes the case for the war against Afrin and welcomes the fact that armed Islamist groups attack peaceful regions in support of Turkey in the latter's neighboring country of Syria. Germany cannot participate in financing such movements."[22]

Its position vis-à-vis Turkey's war has also led to conflicts within the ENKS. While one of the two "future movements" that broke away in 2011 turned its back on the ENKS, accusing the Council of having known about the planned attack on Afrin and doing nothing to prevent it, in February a representative of the other "future movement" in the ENKS's Committee for International Relations, Siamend Hajo, was suspended because he had participated in an anti-PKK conference of the pro-government Turkish think tank SETA in Ankara that same month.[23]

Conversely, the PYD and the YPG rejected the ENKS offer to deploy its own troops (the so-called Roj Peshmerga) to defend Afrin. In a similar vein, the party chairman of the PDKS, Abdelrehman Apo, who had been in jail since July 2017, was not released before Afrin fell and was later handed over to the Syrian secret service.

---

22 Kamal Sido, "Syrien: Unterstützung für syrische oppositionelle Gruppen offenlegen," *Pressportal*, February 5, 2018, accessed October 1, 2018, https://www.presseportal.de/pm/29402/3858686.
23 "PYD/PKK Declares Kurdish People 'Enemy' Over Criticism," *Seta*, February 14, 2018, accessed October 1, 2018, https://www.setav.org/en/tag/siamend-hajo/.

Though only very small Kurdish groups predominantly consisting of village protectors from Turkey[24] and Kurdish Islamists have actively fought on the side of Turkey,[25] the uncompromising character of the conflict among the big Kurdish political forces has certainly done massive damage to the self-administration in Afrin. The reason for this irreconcilability must be sought less in the local political conditions in Afrin or the certainly very real ideological differences, but rather in the political and financial dependency of most of the relevant political forces on actors abroad. The PYD ruling in Afrin until 2018 is the daughter of a Turkish-Kurdish party, and its main rival, the PDKS, was actually founded by Masoud Barzani's PDK in Iraq. Between these poles, local parties can at best position themselves on one or the other side of the line of conflict in order to retain at least a minimum of influence. Thus, the conflicts between the respective mother parties often have an immediate influence on the local and regional level.

Concretely, these conflicts generally play out among the functionaries of the Kurdish parties. However, during the war, the ordinary population, even families whose members are more or less anti- PYD, for the most part maintained solidarity with the population of Afrin and the YPG and YPJ fighters against the Turkish invaders.

Battle for the Border Regions

At the beginning of the war, Erdoğan had grandiloquently claimed that he would take Afrin in half a day. In the early weeks of the Turkish attack on Afrin it seemed that the "commander in chief" had underestimated his opponents. From a Turkish perspective, the first four weeks of the attack on the Kurdish region of Afrin in the north of Syria unfolded relatively

---

24 Kurdish paramilitary force used against the PKK in Turkey since the 1980s.
25 Both Pro-Turkish journalists and sources close to the PYD mentioned the Descendants of Saladin Brigade (Arabic: Liwa aḥfād Ṣalāḥ ad-Dīn, Kurdish: Ketaib Selahedîn El-Eyûbî), the Mashaal Tammo Brigade (Kurdish: Ketîbeya Mişel Temo), the Kurdish Front (Kurdish: Siqûr El-Ekrad), and the Azadî Brigade (Kurdish: Ketîbeya Azadî) as Kurdish groups allegedly fighting on the side of the Turkish army. Of these groups, only the Azadî Brigade and the Descendants of Saladin Brigade had something in the range of several hundred fighters each, while the other groups each consisted of just a handful of mercenaries and village protectors. For its part, the Descendants of Saladin Brigade was actually dissolved in the summer of 2017, and thereafter only consisted of a quickly reassembled remnant of the previous unit.

slowly. In the first few days, the Turkish army and its allies didn't manage to conquer a single village. It was only at the end of the first week that the first villages were captured. By the end of January, the Turkish troops and their allies had captured 11 of the 366 villages in the region. Almost the entire population of these border villages fled to the town of Afrin.

Though in the second and the third weeks of the war, the Turkish army and its Syrian militias succeeded in taking some additional villages, at first, they didn't get much closer to the city of Afrin. On the contrary, the YPG/YPJ was even able to reconquer some of the villages that had been occupied by the Turkish army. In the hilly regions bordering Turkey, the local fighters enjoyed many advantages over the attackers because of their knowledge of the territory and their high motivation. Thus, during the first month of the war, one of the strongest NATO armies, equipped with German tanks, a modern artillery, and drone technology, apparently could achieve no more than an advance of four to six kilometers [two to four miles] into Syrian national territory. Though the Turkish air attacks repeatedly hit fighters of the Kurdish People's Protection Units (YPG) and the Women's Protection Units (YPJ), as well as civilians, four weeks after the beginning of the war the Turkish army was still about eighteen kilometers [eleven miles] from the Afrin city limits.

The Turkish problems in Afrin primarily had to do with the underestimation of Turkey's opponents and the overestimation of its allies. While the Kurdish YPG/YPF units were highly motivated, locally rooted militias, Turkey's jihadist and political Islamic allies came from other regions of Syria, were badly trained, and had little motivation to die for the Turkish war aims in Syria. Conflicts between Turkish units and their Syrian allies that erupted in late January showed that the coordination between the Turkish army and its Syrian ancillary troops was not optimal.

In early February, negotiations between the YPG/YPJ and the Syrian regime that were aimed at allowing fighters of the former to be brought to Afrin through government held territory finally took place. On February 6, the first convoy of YPG/YPJ fighters from the eastern Kurdish areas of Kobanê and Cizîrê reached Afrin through areas under the control of the regime. Apart from YPG and YPJ troops, among the fighters there were also contingents of the Resistance Units of Şingal (Yekîneyên Berxwedana Şengalê, YBŞ) and the Women's Units of Êzidxan (Yekinêyen Jinên Êzidxan, YJÊ), and two Êzîdî units from the Iraqi Sinjar (Kurdish: Şingal).

Then, on February 18, an agreement between the regime and the YPG/ YPJ was announced, according to which Syrian troops were to come to the support of the Kurds without the latter having to transfer the political administration of the canton to the regime. However, this agreement was implemented only in a very limited way. Even though Shiite militias loyal to the government arrived to reinforce the YPG/YPJ during the following days, no Syrian government troops ever showed up. Whether unequivocal threats by Turkey, a Russian veto, or the regime's ultimate strategic considerations were the reason for this hesitation cannot be determined at this point. It is clearly true that these Shiite militias were useful but could only slow down not stop the advance of the Turkish army.

It remains unclear whether the advance of the Turkish army was accompanied by the use of prohibited chemical weapons, as was claimed by the Kurdish side but denied by the Turks.[26]

Advance of the Turkish Troops

Despite the support by Shiite militias, in the second half of February the YPG and the YPJ came under increasing military pressure. The region was successively encircled and under siege. More and more civilians were forced to seek refuge in the city of Afrin. Finally, on February 22, the YPG had to withdraw from the Kurdish district of Aleppo in order to support the struggle in Afrin.

On February 28, the UN Security Council unanimously adopted Resolution 2401, calling on all war parties[27] in Syria to implement a cease-fire of at least thirty days to enable humanitarian aid. Turkey clearly stated that it would disregard the resolution and continue its war on Afrin. After an increase in territorial gains by Turkey in the second half of February, more and more civilians from the contested villages and the villages captured by Turkey and its allies fled to the city of Afrin. This was accompanied by a tendency of the middle class in Afrin to migrate to Aleppo or the other Kurdish areas further to the east.

---

26 "Turkey Denies Use of Chemical Weapons in Syria," *DW.com*, February 17, 2018, accessed October 1, 2018, http://www.dw.com/en/turkey-denies-use-of-chemical-weapons-in-syria/a-42627819.

27 The only explicit exceptions were attacks against the IS and al-Qaeda, that is, the Hai'at Tahrīr ash-Shām.

According to reports, by March, several thousand civilians had already fled to Aleppo and in the direction of Qamişlo. That route, however, passed through areas under the control of Shiite militias from both Syria and Iran and was only safe for refugees smuggled by the Shiite militias from Nubl and az-Zahrā'. In early March, these militias demanded between eight hundred and a thousand dollars per person, a price that, given the economic situation in Afrin and the size of the average family, is for many simply unaffordable.

Between March 2 and March 5, Turkish troops captured their first regional capital, Reco. After a bombardment lasting for days, they also took the second largest city in the region, Cindirês. At the time, the overwhelming majority of the inhabitants had already left both towns in the direction of Afrin.

On March 6, the Kurdish and Arab organizations in the Syrian Democratic Forces announced that in the future they would take a defensive position concerning the remnants of the Islamic State, because they had to withdraw troops from the southeast in order to defend Afrin.[28] Altogether, at that point, 1,700 fighters were withdrawn from the front against the IS. Thus, the IS, which at the time only controlled a stretch of about thirty kilometers [eighteen miles] on the northern side of the Euphrates valley, reaching from the town of Hajin to the Iraqi border, and was on the brink of military collapse was given a new lease on life and possibly even a chance to consolidate itself at a reduced level. Be that as it may, for the time being the struggle against the IS had come to an end, because all military resources were needed for to defend Afrin.

About six months after the beginning of the war, both sides published intermediate assessments that could not have been more different. While the Turkish president Erdoğan, at the March 6 cornerstone laying ceremony for the new Supreme Court of Turkey building, claimed that "2,878 terrorists" had been "neutralized"[29]—the language used by Turkey for the killing of YPG/YPJ fighters—since the beginning of the war, on the following day the YPG declared that since the beginning of the fighting, 283

---

28 "Revolutionary Forces: We Will Send Our Forces to Afrin," AFN News, March 7, 2018, accessed October 1, 2018, https://anfenglish.com/news/revolutionary-forces-we-will-send-our-forces-to-afrin-25328.

29 "Erdoğan: Afrin'de etkisiz hale getirilen terörist sayısı 2878 oldu," Türkiye, March 6, 2018, accessed October 1, 2018, http://www.turkiyegazetesi.com.tr/gundem/548486.aspx.

of its fighters had "been martyred during direct engagements and heroic resistance against the terrorist invaders."[30] According to the YPG balance sheet, 165 civilians including 28 women and children were killed by the bomb attacks and Turkish artillery fire, and 650 civilians were wounded. The YPG further claimed to have killed "1,588 members of the terrorist factions and Turkish soldiers," among them 11 Turkish soldiers, who had lost their lives when two helicopters were shot down.

These numbers from Turkish and Kurdish sources diverge sharply, and there were no independent observers on the battlefield. Other institutions were also forced to rely on information from the local war parties. On March 9, the London-based Syrian Observatory for Human Rights, which is politically close to the moderate Sunni opposition and tends to sympathize with the groups on the side of Turkey but is not directly linked to any of the war parties in Afrin, published a balance sheet that was much soberer than those produced by the two war parties. It claimed that since the beginning of the war 409 fighters on the Turkish side had been killed, including 71 Turkish soldiers, the rest of the dead having been fighters in the various militias. According to the Observatory, the YPG lost 359 fighters, while the regime-controlled National Defense Forces, essentially the Shiite militias, lost 81 fighters since entering the war on the side of the YPG on February 20. The Observatory talked about 204 Syrian civilians of Kurdish, Arab, and Armenian descent killed, including 32 children.[31]

In general, one could assume that the war parties would try to downplay the numbers of their own casualties, while exaggerating those of their enemies. But anyone acquainted with how the YPG and the YPJ deal with their own dead and who has seen the ceremony surrounding martyr funerals in Afrin will agree that the YPG does not hide its casualties. On the contrary, the pictures of the fallen fighters, who are venerated as martyrs, are to be found everywhere in Afrin. The funerals

---

30 "SDF Releases Balance Sheet on Afrin Battle Since January 20," *ANF News*, March 7, 2018, accessed October 6, 2018, https://anfenglish.com/rojava/sdf-releases-balance-sheet-on-afrin-battle-since-january-20-25335.

31 "With the Continued Turkish Killing against People of Afrin Area, Thousands of Civilians Displace from the Area and Stay in the Open with the Increase of the Tragedy of More Than a Million Civilians," *Syrian Observatory for Human Rights*, March 9, 2018, accessed October 6, 2018, http://www.syriahr.com/en/?p=86414.

of YPG and YPJ fighters are celebrated as propaganda exercises, during which even the stores are administratively ordered to close down. One can thus assume that the number given by the YPG of the YPG/YPJ fighters killed was accurate. Moreover, as opposed to the Turkish army, the YPG always provided the exact location and time of the death of its fighters. Whether the number of enemies it claimed to have killed is as precise is open to debate. What, then, explains the enormous difference between the Turkish and the Kurdish numbers?

The Turkish government claimed that there were no civilian casualties in this war. Responding to criticism over the killing of civilians, Erdoğan employed an openly racist undertone in public speeches broadcast on Turkish TV: "You unscrupulous, you shameless, you dishonorable people! It is not us but you who have it in their blood to kill civilians!"

To mask the obvious propaganda lie that Turkey didn't kill civilians, the Turkish side simply counted civilian casualties as "neutralized terrorists." But this alone would not have been sufficient to arrive at the alleged number of 2,878 "neutralized terrorists." The key to this success record probably lay with Turkey's dead allies. The Syrian militias fighting against the YPG/YPJ alongside Turkey were not officially registered anywhere. Nobody really knows who fought in the ranks of the militias that Turkey called the Free Syrian Army, a group that by then actually had very little to do with the groups that had taken up the fight against the Syrian regime under that name back in 2011. They were nothing more than a hodgepodge of more or less Islamist and jihadist rebels, including foreign fighters who had previously signed up with the IS. Turkey, for its part, now claimed to be fighting not just against the YPG but also against the IS. Even though the claim was completely absurd, given that there hadn't been any IS fighters anywhere near Afrin since at least 2016, Turkey could use the death in action of any former IS fighters to support its propaganda. The solution to the riddle therefore seemed to be that Erdoğan simply counted the dead among his Syrian allies as "neutralized terrorists," thereby improving the Turkish army's track record without mentioning that these "terrorists" were casualties on the Turkish side. That said, even if the allied Syrian fighters and the civilians were counted among them, the numbers provided by Erdoğan were probably still extremely exaggerated. The balance sheet of the Syrian Observatory for Human Rights probably provides a more realistic overall picture.

German Arms and German Money

While the Austrian National Assembly adopted an arms embargo against Turkey supported by all parties represented in the parliament in November 2016, to this day Germany continues to export arms and other military equipment to Turkey. Germany not only delivered war materiel in the years leading up to the attack on Afrin, as the Turkish army advanced militarily against Kurdish cities in the southeast of Turkey and was already threatening to attack Afrin, but even after the war against Afrin had begun it continued to grant export permissions. The German minister for economic affairs responded to a question in parliament from the Green member of parliament Omid Nouripour by saying that twenty export permissions for the delivery of German military equipment worth 4.4 million euros to Turkey had been granted during the first five and a half weeks of the war. Only weeks before, in February 2018, the German foreign minister Sigmar Gabriel had repeatedly claimed that a complete export ban for all armaments destined for Turkey had been in force since the beginning of Turkey's Syria offensive.[32] Between 2006 and 2011, Germany delivered 347 so-called Leopard 2 tanks from the Düsseldorf-based arms dealer Rheinmetall to Turkey.[33] At least some of these combat tanks were verifiably used by the Turkish army in its war against Afrin.

While there has been a massive crackdown against Kurdish protests accompanied by warnings against "importing conflicts" into Germany, the country profits handsomely from the Turkey's wars against its own population and the population of Syria. Columnist Schluwa Sama hit the mark when she addressed the Germans recently with the following words: "OK, dear people of Germany, you are not just *complicit* in these crimes because you sell some arms to Turkey. No, your whole lifestyle, your economy, your success as the world champion in exports is based on the export of murder. In 2016, while I was protesting the repression in Turkey, the

---

32 Michael Fischer, "Millionenschwere Rüstungsexporte in die Türkei gehen weiter," *Neues Deutschland*, March 15, 2018, accessed October 1, 2018, https://www.neues-deutschland.de/m/artikel/1082516.syrien-krieg-millionenschwere-ruestungsexporte-in-die-tuerkei-gehen-weiter.amp.html?_twitter_impression=true.

33 Wolfgang Wichmann, "Exportschlager ohne Einsatzbeschränkung," *Tagesschau*, January 23 2018, accessed October 1, 2018, http://faktenfinder.tagesschau.de/inland/leopard-109.html.

German government granted permissions for the export of war materiel to Turkey worth more than ninety-eight million euros."[34]

Germany does not just earn good money with the exports of arms to Turkey, which are then used against Afrin. The European refugee policy also makes its contribution to war and occupation in Afrin.

EU Refugee Policy and the War against Afrin

Europe has a close connection with Afrin not just because of arms exports but also because of its refugee policy. In 2015, governments hostile to refugees, including those in Austria or Hungary, tried to convince Turkey to close the escape routes from Syria, Iraq, and Afghanistan through Turkey into the EU. On November 29, 2015, representatives of the EU and Turkey activated the October 15 EU-Turkey Joint Action Plan to limit immigration via Turkey, which included a pledge of up to three billion euros for Turkey and assigned it the task of preventing refugees from continuing their journey into the EU and taking back refugees who had managed to make the dangerous voyage across the sea to one of the Greek islands.

On March 18, 2016, the European Union concluded an agreement with Turkey that provided for an accelerated payment of the envisaged three billion euros and the replenishment of this sum by an additional three billion euros before the end of 2018. Then, on June 1, 2016, the EU-Turkey Readmission Agreement of December 16, 2013, came into full effect within the framework of the provisions of the new EU-Turkey Agreement of 2016.[35]

On the one hand, the agreement left the EU increasingly open to Turkish blackmail, because the latter could always threaten to "unleash" the refugees the EU was so afraid of. At the same time, however, it led to a growing backlog of refugees in Turkey. In 2012, Turkey had accepted the largest number of refugees from Syria, a fact that had already led to substantial social and political tensions in some of the border regions. These

---

34 Schluwa Sama, "Der Mordexportweltmeister sorgt sich um importierte Konflikte," *Alsharq*, March 2, 2018, accessed October 1, 2018, http://www.alsharq.de/2018/gesellschaft/der-mordexportweltmeister-sorgt-sich-um-importierte-konflikte/.

35 "Cecilia Malmström Signs the Readmission Agreement and Launches the Visa Liberalisation Dialogue with Turkey," *European Commission Press Release Database*, December 16, 2013, accessed October 1, 2018, http://europa.eu/rapid/press-release_IP-13-1259_en.htm.

tensions were exacerbated because the Turkish government instrumentalized for its own political power purposes the many conservative Sunni refugees, among whom were many loyal adherents of Erdoğan's political line. Turkey tried to keep the refugees in regions where the AKP had many opponents, such as the Kurdish border regions or the province Hatay, which is strongly dominated by Arabic-speaking Alevi. It was no accident that both are areas with many leftist and secular opponents of the AKP.

Since the March 2016 agreement with the EU, the number of Syrian refugees in Turkey has increased quite substantially. On March 8, 2018, the UN Refugee Agency, the United Nations High Commissioner for Refugees (UNHCR), said that there were 3,547,194 registered Syrian refugees in Turkey,[36] which was one million more than at the beginning of 2016! Obviously, the EU border regime and the agreement with Turkey has led to an additional backlog of refugees in Turkey, many of whom want to travel to Europe but are forced to remain in Turkey because of the Turkish-European cooperation in erecting a defense wall against refugees.

To the Syrian refugees in Turkey we must add the refugees from Iran and Iraq and those originally from Afghanistan who, because of the European-Turkish anti-refugee policy, are also stuck in Turkey. At the beginning of the "refugee deal," 125 thousand Iraqi asylum seekers, 120 thousand Afghan asylum seekers, and 30 thousand Iranian asylum seekers were stuck in Turkey, numbers that have since increased. In many regions of Turkey, this extremely high aggregate number of refugees—altogether almost four million people—has turned into a genuine social and economic problem, a problem for which there is no simple solution, because the situation in Syria has not yet calmed down and there is now a lack of escape routes to Europe.

The fact that the EU is buying the closure of the borders by financially supporting Turkey not only makes the EU susceptible to blackmail but also intensifies the problems in Turkey. This has contributed to Turkey's decision to conquer Afrin. In doing so the Turkish regime is not just concerned with domestic political power objectives and the destruction of de facto Kurdish autonomy but also with the repatriation of the refugees to Syria.

36　United Nations High Commissioner for Refugees, "Syria Regional Refugee Response," September 21, 2018, accessed October 1, 2018, https://data2.unhcr.org/en/situations/syria/location/113.

Ethnic Cleansing: Arabization and Turkmenization

Turkey made it plain from the beginning that one of the goals of the war against Afrin was the "readmission" of half a million Syrian refugees to Afrin. In mid-February 2018, the president's wife, Emine Erdoğan, publicly announced in a speech in Istanbul that "nearly 500,000 people are expected to return to Afrin" after the Turkish conquest.[37] This speech was widely circulated in the Turkish press and was noted internationally at the time. But the notion of a "readmission" can be confidently described as a propaganda lie, because until Turkey's attack on the Kurdish enclave there had been hardly any refugees from Afrin in Turkey. The five hundred thousand Syrians whom the government in Ankara wants to settle in Afrin come from completely different areas in Syria and are not Kurdish but are predominantly Arab. Moreover, before the Syrian war the number of inhabitants of all of Afrin wasn't even close to five hundred thousand. Thus, the first lady's pronouncement, which was subsequently repeated by a number of officials, was actually nothing but an open threat of impending ethnic cleansing.

The aim of Turkey is not to just conquer Afrin but also to expel or kill the Kurdish population that had already been living in this region centuries before the emergence of the Ottoman Empire and that gave the "Mountain of the Kurds" its name, to obliterate the Kurdish language and culture in this region, and to settle pro-Turkish Arab and Turkmen settlers there.

Most of the civilians fled from the villages when the Turkish army approached. There have been reports from several villages where people have been prevented from returning. In cases where villagers were unable or unwilling to flee on time, they were sometimes brutally murdered. A video depicting a peasant who refused to relinquish his tractor to the pro-Turkish militias and was immediately shot circulated on social media, as did photos of other atrocities perpetrated against civilians. At any rate, the Turkish army's jihadist allies are now so feared that only a few civilians remain in the villages, creating room for the Turkish government resettlement program.

---

37 "500,000 Syrians will 'return to Afrin' after fighting ends, says Turkey's First Lady," *The Arab News*, February 18, 2018, accessed October 2, 2018, https://www.alaraby.co.uk/english/news/2018/2/18/500-000-syrians-will-return-to-afrin-turkeys-first-lady.

To mislead the international public about what is really going on in the run-up to the Arabization and Turkmenization of the region Erdoğan had personally claimed that Afrin's population was in fact 55 percent Arab, 7 percent Turkmen, and only 35 percent Kurdish, adding that he wanted to give the land "back to its rightful owners."[38]

Turkey apparently felt certain that this plan would not meet with any relevant international protest. So, on March 15, an official spokesperson for the Turkish government openly declared that the Turkish government had no intention of returning Afrin to the Syrian government and that Turkey intended to rule the town in the future.[39]

The battles in the city of Afrin had hardly even started in March 2018 when the first Arab and Turkmen settlers were brought in and given the houses of the civilian population that had fled the villages conquered by Turkey and its allies. Some of the first families settled there were relatives of fighters in the pro-Turkish militias, along with Arabs from various Syrian cities and Turkmens from Iraq who had cooperated with the so-called Islamic State. Even before the attack on Afrin, Sunni Turkmens from the city of Tal Afar had appeared in the region around A'zaz held by the Turkish army and pro-Turkish militias.

In 2014, when the IS took Tal Afar, many Sunni Turkmens in this almost exclusively Turkmen city had assaulted their Shiite Turkmen neighbors, stolen their property, and raped their daughters. Not all of them participated, however, and some of them also fled from the massacres of the IS and the murderous anti-Shiite policy of the jihadists. But the collaboration of a substantial number of Sunni Turkmens, coupled with fact that a number of them held high positions within the IS and had a particularly evil reputation,[40] only served to intensify the already existing confessionalized

---

38 "Erdogan says Afrin Is Majority Arab, Threatens Arabization," *Kurdistan 24*, January 21, 2018, accessed October 1, 2018, http://www.kurdistan24.net/en/news/7899b6c9-f475-40fb-a9bc-ffda4b69f0df.

39 Andrew Illingworth, "Turkey Will Not Hand Over Afrin to Syrian Government After Seizing It—Erdogan's spokesperson," *AMN*, March 15, 2018, accessed November 3, 2018, https://www.almasdarnews.com/article/breaking-turkey-will-not-hand-over-afrin-to-syrian-government-after-seizing-it-erdogans-spokesperson/.

40 Between 2014 and 2017, stories about such particularly notorious IS commanders in Tal Afar were widespread among the displaced persons from the region. These stories were not just told by Shiites from Tal Afar, but also by Christians and Êzîdî. Among others, Patrick Cockburn wrote in the *Independent* on

perception of the conflict. The Shiite Turkmens from Tal Afar either fled to Kurdistan or, at first, to the Êzîdî in Sinjar (Kurdish: Şingal), from where they had again to flee from the IS in August 2014. If they were not killed by the IS, just like the other religious minorities in the region around Mosul— the Christians, the Kakai and Shabak from the Nineveh plain, and the Êzîdî from Sinjar—they eventually found themselves in the camps for displaced persons around Erbil or Dohuk. In conversations with Turkmens from Tal Afar, one would quickly hear that it was now impossible to live together with "these monsters." The Sunnis were regarded as abusers, and many of the refugees mentioned their neighbors by name and described the crimes they had committed. In Tal Afar, the IS did not represent an alien army, but consisted of Sunni neighbors and friends who now attacked and savaged their Shiite fellow citizens. With the reconquest of Tal Afar by the Iraqi army and Shiite militias, the only realistic option for the Sunni Turkmens still in the city was to flee. The IS had poisoned the situation to such an extent that it was now either/or: them or us. The Sunni Turkmens finally ended up in the region around A'zaz or in Turkey, but in the latter case, they did not receive Syrian refugee status nor were they regarded as Turks.[41]

Now the Turkish government obviously sees the opportunity to get rid of these unwelcome guests, while simultaneously destroying the Kurdish character of the Kurd Dagh and creating a perceived reality that will not be easy to reverse in the future. As the Arabization policies of both Saddam Hussein in Kirkuk and the Syrian regime in the 1960s in the

---

November 15, 2016: "'Isis is full of killers, but the worst killers of all come from Tal Afar,' says a senior Iraqi official who did not want his name published. Abbas, a 47-year-old Shia Turkmen from Tal Afar living in exile in the Kurdish city of Zakho, agrees, saying that several of the senior military commanders of the self-declared Caliph Abu Bakr al-Baghdadi come from there. He adds that officers from the Shia paramilitaries have been told that they will soon attack the city. The Turkmen are one of Iraq's smaller minorities but important because of their links to Isis and to Turkey." Patrick Cockburn, "'Isis is Full of Killers, the Worst Come from Tal Afar': Bitter Fight for City Ahead and the Violence May Not End There," November 15, 2016, accessed October 2, 2018, http://www.independent.co.uk/news/world/middle-east/isis-mosul-offensive-latest-tal-afar-killers-iraq-sectarian-violence-a7419536.html.

41 Suraj Sharma, "Iraq's Turkmen, the Refugees Created and Forgotten by Everyone," September 1, 2017, accessed October 2, 2018, http://www.middleeasteye.net/news/iraq-s-turkmen-refugees-created-and-forgotten-everyone-134794379.

Cizîrê show, such resettlements can contribute to ethnic conflicts decades later. In the case of Afrin, the expulsion of the Kurdish population and the colonization of the region by Arab and Turkmen settlers represent a particularly perfidious strategy. Of course, the Turkish authorities know perfectly well that the Kurdish population will never simply accept being expelled from a key Kurdish area such as Afrin, and that it regards the settlers now moving into its houses, not entirely unjustifiably, as part of the military aggression against the Kurds. Erdoğan's brazen lies about an Arab majority and a substantial Turkmen minority in the region are setting the stage for a later narrative about the Kurds attacking innocent civilians when they resist the new settlers.

Indeed, on March 13, 2018, the YPG command in Afrin issued a statement warning Turkey against any "settlement of families of the gangs that act with the invading Turkish state" in the villages Kurds had fled or been expelled from. According to the statement, Turkmens from A'zaz, Atmeh, Turkey, and Iraq had already been settled in the regions of Şiye and Cindirês. The statement further said that these groups had been brought to the Kurdish villages and cities in violation of international law and were thus regarded as legitimate targets by the YPG.[42]

It is obvious that Turkey not only envisages a genocidal expulsion of the Kurdish population, but that it also consciously includes future ethnic conflicts in its calculations. It is apparently so sure of itself in all of this that it has openly announced this ethnic cleansing—and indeed, neither

---

42 In the English translation by the ANF news agency, which is close to the PKK, the end of the statement reads: "We in the YPG state clearly that the regions where the invading Turkish state is changing the demographic structure have been a battle field since the first day and military activities have been taking in these regions up until now. We warn those who are an instrument to or have a part in the Turkish state's scheme not to approach these regions. In contrary case, they will be a target to the legitimate aims of our fighters. We also call on those that become an instrument to this dirty scheme to not be deceived by the Turkish state's schemes. We also warn them not to put support behind the Turkish state's hostile practices against the local people because the settlement in the regions that have been invaded without a consideration of any law or legitimacy will be realized by use of force, which will constitute a violation of international laws and it is a most incontestable right for our fighters to target these regions." "YPG: Those Coming to Afrin with Turkey Will Be Our Target," *ANF News*, March 14, 2018, accessed October 2, 2018, https://anfenglish.com/rojava/ypg-those-coming-to-afrin-with-turkey-will-be-our-target-25464.

its NATO partners nor Russia have registered any meaningful protests. For Erdoğan, this must have looked like a free pass for proceeding with his endeavor.

The Attack on the City of Afrin

By March 6, the Turkish troops and their allies had already advanced toward the city of Afrin. From that date on, mobile phones in the city stopped working, because the Turkish military had done such extensive damage to the cell towers. The Meydanke dam, which holds a large part of the city's water supply, was attacked several times and was damaged so severely that after March 8, the town's water supply largely collapsed.

After the conquest of Cindirês on March 9, the Turkish troops and their allies advanced toward Afrin from the southwest, beginning a pincer attack on the region's capital. At that time, there were at least three times as many civilians in the town as usual, because the regular population had been augmented by the refugees from the villages and small towns that were already in the hands of Turkish troops.

Beginning on March 10, the Turkish Air Force bombarded the city, hitting not only YPG/YPJ military positions but also residential housing. On March 12, Turkish troops reached the city limits, converging from two sides. But Turkish reports that the city was completely encircled turned out to be premature. Until March 15, the city was still accessible from the southeast and the northwest, even though Turkish units were firing on the access routes, turning the flight from the city into a dangerous undertaking. Nevertheless, on March 13, an increasing number of civilians began fleeing southeast, trying to reach areas under government control. Though it is difficult to provide accurate numbers, from talking to civilians in the region I could ascertain that until March 16 it was possible to flee the city, and that the YPG—contrary to Turkish claims—did not prevent the civilians from fleeing. On the other hand, a substantial part of the civilian population did not want to leave the town, either because they feared they would never be able to return, or because they regarded an escape under Turkish fire as just as dangerous as simply remaining in the town. Be that as it may, by March 17, around two hundred thousand civilians had fled.[43]

---

43 "Hundreds of Civilians Flee as Turkish Forces Advance on Syria's Afrin City," *France 24*, accessed November 3, 2018, https://www.france24.com/en/20180312-syria-afrin-city-hundreds-civilians-flee-turkish-forces.

However, because of the influx of those expelled from the villages in the weeks before the attack on the city, it is next to impossible to say how many civilians remain in the town at this point. As of May 2018, a number of residences were still inhabited by several parties. Thus, the town probably still harbored many more civilians than before the beginning of the war.

During the night of March 15, there were targeted bombardments of residential areas that, according to Kurdish reports, killed eleven people and wounded many more.[44] On March 16, the town's hospital, which had provided emergency care for the wounded during the previous days, was bombed by the Turkish Air Force. According to Kurdish sources, at least fifteen people were killed during the attack. Altogether, according to Kurdish reports, forty-seven civilians died during this indiscriminate Turkish army attack on what was bloodiest day of the invasion up to that point.[45]

On March 17, the bombardment of the town continued, with more civilian casualties. At the same time, thousands of additional civilians fled in the direction of Syrian government–held areas. On the midmorning of March 18, the YPG/YPJ finally withdrew from the city. Even though a statement said that the struggle had reached "another stage" and was not over, it also said that to avoid a civilian massacre the YPG had decided to evacuate them from the town. It added that 500 civilians and 820 SDF fighters had been killed since the beginning of fighting.[46] Pictures of Turkish tanks on the main square and the replacement of Kurdish flags by Turkish ones on official buildings were disseminated via Twitter, making it clear that the city had fallen into the hands of the Turkish army and its allies by midmorning.

The reasons for the surprisingly quick withdrawal from the city and the avoidance of any fighting in the urban areas themselves remained unclear. The official version of the YPG/YPJ continued to be that this was to enable a civilian retreat and limit civilian casualties as much as possible. Within the YPG and the PKK, however, there were discussions

---

44 Information Center of Afrin Resistance—Weekly Bulletin 5, March 8–15, 2018.

45 "Turkish Attacks Kill 47 Civilians in Afrin in One Day," *ANF News*, March 17, 2018, accessed October 2, 2018, https://anfenglish.com/rojava/turkish-attacks-kill-47-civilians-in-afrin-25536.

46 "Afrin Administration: The War Has Moved to Another Stage," *AFN News*, March 18, 2018, accessed October 2, 2018, https://anfenglish.com/rojava/afrin-administration-the-war-has-moved-to-another-stage-25570.

about extent to which Öcalan might have directly exerted his influence to accelerate the abandonment of the city. There are two variations on this speculation: on the one hand, there were persistent rumors that a Russian and/or Turkish delegation visited Öcalan on the prison island of Imralı and pressured him to order the withdrawal of the YPG from Afrin; on the other hand, there was also a supposition that Öcalan wanted to use the withdrawal as a way to get back into the game. But all of this remains speculation, and it is by no means clear that Öcalan was in any way directly involved in this decision, given that the PKK leader has been almost completely isolated on Imralı since 1999 and for the most part can only communicate with the Kurdish movement in general and the de facto leadership of the PKK around Murat Karayılan in particular through his lawyers—and he hasn't seen his lawyers since 2011!

Reports of YPG fighters who had remained in Afrin until March 18 gave the impression that toward the end the situation in the town was increasingly chaotic, that many of the fighters didn't have clear orders, and that many of the communication channels had apparently broken down.

It can certainly be said that even though the YPG could have raised the ante for Turkey's conquest of the city by engaging in street battles, the price would probably have been the destruction of the city and many civilian deaths. To prevent the seizure of the city without the support of any true allies would presumably have been impossible. Thus, the decision to withdraw from the city—whoever actually took it—probably did prevent an even worse bloodbath and allow the refugees to flee.

The Battle for the Last Rural Areas

On March 17, the Turkish army reached Mabeta, the center of the Alevi minority in the canton of Afrin. Like Afrin, Mabeta was captured on March 18. By that evening, the YPG/YPJ fighters only controlled a few rural areas in the center of the region and in the predominantly Êzîdî area in the far southeast of the canton. In May 2018, it was still not clear whether these villages would be taken by the Syrian or the Turkish army. For the Êzîdî minority, the conquest of their villages by the Turkish army would probably be far worse than a takeover by the Syrian army, not least because of the Turkish army's jihadist allies.

Though there was still fighting in the central hill lands of the canton for a few days after the fall of the city of Afrin, with the loss of the latter it had become clear that for the time being the Turkish army and its allies had won the war. Several days after the fall of the town of Afrin, the Turkish army and its allies ended their final offensive in the southeast of Afrin with the conquest of Basûfanê, Bircê Hêdrê, and some nearby Êzîdî villages. By April 2018, the YPG/YPJ was only able to hold its ground in a few mountain villages in the far southeast of the region, on the mountain plain of the Çiyayê Lêlûn between Fatritin, Bircilqasê, and Meyasê.

In the second half of April 2018, much less was heard about a guerilla war than had been the case in the first two weeks following the capture of the city of Afrin. Even in rural Afrin, there do not seem to be any organized YPG or YPJ units at this point. By mid-April 2018, a stable front line had reemerged between the YPG/YPJ and the Turkish army and its allies with almost the whole Kurdish region of Afrin under Turkish occupation. Apart from Fatritin, Bircilqasê, and Meyasê, there were areas around Tal Rifaat in the east of Afrin that had been captured in 2016 that were under the joint control of Syrian government troops and the YPG/YPJ.

The Situation in the Province Şehba and at the Çiyayê Lêlûn

Despite Turkish President Erdoğan's repeated announcements that Turkey would also conquer Tal Rifaat, this region—which the Democratic Federation of Northern Syria describes as part of the province of Şehba— has not yet been attacked. For the YPG, this thirty-kilometer-long [nineteen-mile] and ten-kilometer-wide [six-mile] strip, which was only conquered by the YPG/YPJ and its Arab allies in 2016, and which has a very mixed population, with an Arab majority and Kurdish and Turkmen minorities, forms, along with the geographically separate Manbij, the province of Şehba, which, in turn, with the province of Afrin, has constituted the region of Afrin (Herêma Efrînê) since Democratic Federation of Northern Syria administrative reform of 2017.

The town Tal Rifaat with its approximately twenty thousand inhabitants was the political center of the region and was once predominantly Arab, but the mass flight from Afrin it made it the most important haven for Kurdish refugees. Of the total of 200 thousand displaced persons in May 2018, around 150 thousand were in the area around Tal Rifaat, which is difficult to reach even for aid organizations. Only the Kurdish Red Crescent had access, and it was able to build an emergency infrastructure in the first weeks after the fall of Afrin.

There were efforts underway to reintegrate the refugees into the political structure of the Democratic Federation of Northern Syria by means of refugee councils. But because international journalists had no access to the region, an enclave sandwiched between the regime and the Turkish forces, information about the region is not terribly reliable.

Were the Turkish government to capture this enclave, the situation faced by refugees would be even more difficult. But the presence of Russian soldiers and units of the Syrian government army alongside the units of the YPG/YPJ and its allies seems to indicate that Russia hasn't given Turkey the go-ahead to attack Şehba and apparently envisages this region under Syrian government control in the long run.

Apart from the region of Tal Rifaat, a few Êzîdî villages on the massif of Çiyayê Lêlûn have also remained under the control of the YPG/YPJ. These villages around Fatritin, Bircilqasê, and Meyasê are located in a barely accessible mountain range immediately next to the Arab-Shiite enclave of Nubl and az-Zahrā', which is held by the Syrian regime and is probably of no great strategic interest to the Turkish side. Even though these last remaining villages in the region of Afrin have not experienced any expulsions, the situation there is undoubtedly very dangerous and uncertain. They too have become havens for displaced persons from the nearby regions. In addition to the constant fear that Turkey and its allies might decide to advance even further, these villages are now cut off from all their markets and have no choice but to be self-sufficient.

Afrin after the Turkish Conquest

Since the Turkish conquest of the city, the situation in Afrin has been extremely precarious. The fact that the Turkish occupiers don't allow independent journalists into the region should set off alarm bells, as it makes verifying the news coming from the Kurdish side about massive abuses of the civilian population very difficult. For example, rumors about kidnappings, forced conversions of Êzîdî, extrajudicial executions, and rapes cannot be accurately assessed. On the other hand, it is not only sources close to the YPG who talk about these practices but also refugees who still have some very limited contact with relatives in the region.

At least one Êzîdî cemetery in the village of Gundê Feqîra was desecrated and partially destroyed. The defiling of individual Êzîdî graves, as well as Muslim graves with Kurdish inscriptions, was also reported in a number of other places. In the city of Afrin, the Mala Êzîdiya, a religious and social center established by Êzîdî close to the PYD, and the statue of the prophet Zoroaster that had been placed in front of it, were destroyed.

In July 2018, In the village of Basûfanê, which until March 2018 was inhabited almost exclusively by Êzîdî, and in whose surroundings a number of early Christian church ruins are to be found, the house of a sixty-year-old Êzîdî was confiscated by the pro-Turkish Ahfad al-Rasul Brigade, which was originally financed by Qatar, and converted into a Sunni mosque. The mosque is now used to give Quran lessons that the children of the Êzîdî are forced to attend. The goal is to alienate them from their parents and to convert them to Islam.

There is clear proof that there has been systematic plundering of the houses of the those expelled, and that there have been at least individual kidnappings and rapes, as well as forced conversions of Êzîdî. How systematic these practices are and whether they reflect the policy of the Turkish army or simply represent excesses by its jihadist allies has not yet been independently verified. Even if these practices were "only" excesses of individual jihadist militias and were not condoned by the Turkish army or government, the latter are still politically responsible for them. After all, it was these bodies that decided to attack the Kurds in Afrin with these particular allies.

At any rate, the Turkish occupiers are preparing for a prolonged presence in the region. School is now based on the Turkish curriculum, pictures published in the Turkish media show students in Afrin being obliged to salute the Turkish flag, and Turkish flags and pictures of Turkey's President Erdoğan hang in the schools in the region.

With the creation of an Afrin Council, chaired by a Kurdish spokesperson Hasan Şindi, in late March, Turkey established a civilian administrative body that, though predominantly staffed by Kurds, does not enjoy any legitimacy in the region. Apart from the eleven Kurds, the council includes eight Arabs and one Turkmen and operates from the Turkish town of Gaziantep.[47] Because Hasan Şindi had in the past been close to the ENKS, the PYD and the YPG have accused the latter of collaborating with the occupiers. Even though the ENKS and its member parties have not, at least officially, participated in the Turkish Afrin Council, at the beginning of April a "people's court" in Qamişlo issued an arrest warrant against the two top officials of the Yekîtî Party, Fûad Elîko and Ibrehîm Biro, accusing

47 "Turkish-Backed Interim Council Elected in Afrin: State Media," *Rûdaw*, April 12, 2018, accessed October 2, 2018, http://www.rudaw.net/english/middleeast/syria/120420183.

them of "treason against the achievements of the Kurdish people."[48] For his part, Fûad Elîko told the Iraqi-Kurdish broadcaster Rûdaw, part of the pro-Barzani media, that the ruling Rojava parties had endangered the Kurdish people with their policies, which enabled the Turkish government to occupy Afrin. He said that for him the biggest problem was the demographic changes in Afrin planned by Turkey, and he claimed to be working "day and night to ensure the return of our nation."[49]

This is not the place to decide whether members of the ENKS who are trying to use diplomatic means to get Turkey to withdraw from Afrin and to specifically allow those expelled to return should be evaluated as collaboration, which is how the PYD and the YPG see it, but it is clear that the loss the YPG suffered in Afrin has intensified its conflict with the ENKS, and it has been looking for "Kurdish collaborators" to blame—some might also say, excuse—its defeat. At any rate, it is surely true that even though certain individual Kurds on the so-called Afrin Council cooperate with the Turkish occupiers, these persons are neither representatives of Kurdish parties participating in the ENKS nor are they otherwise relevant in the region. At least officially, the ENKS also speaks of an occupation of Afrin in violation of international law. Thus, despite the intensification of the internal Kurdish tensions, all important Kurdish forces agree that it is necessary to enable the return of those expelled and to have Turkey withdraw. Up until May, the Turkish army and its allies systematically prevented those expelled from returning to Afrin.

According to UN estimates, at the end of April about fifty to seventy thousand civilians remained in the city of Afrin, living under the strict occupation of Islamist militias who try to enforce "Islamic" dress codes for women and to prevent religious minorities from practicing their religion. The houses of those expelled have been occupied by Arab and Turkmen settlers coming from East Ghouta—which has by now been captured by the regime—and whose settlement the Turkish regime tries to sell as a "return of refugees." In reality, these people originally come from

---

48 "People's Court Issues Arrest Warrants for two ENKS Members," *ANF News*, April 6, 2018, accessed October 2, 2018, https://anfenglishmobile.com/rojava-northern-syria/people-s-court-issues-arrest-warrants-for-two-enks-members-25949.

49 "Rojava Rulers Call on Rival Kurdish Movement to Leave Pro-Turkish Coalition," *Rûdaw*, March 23, 2018, accessed October 2, 2018, http://www.rudaw.net/english/middleeast/syria/23032018.

other parts of Syria, or even from Iraq, and have no relationship whatsoever with Afrin. On April 11, the deputy director general of the Turkish Ministry of the Interior's immigration authority, Abdullah Ayaz, said that "around 162,000 Syrian refugees have returned to the areas liberated during Operation Euphrates Shield and Operation Olive Branch."[50] This refers not only to Afrin, but also to the regions between Kobanê and Afrin captured by the Turkish army and its allies in 2016. But if even half of this number was brought to Afrin, this is enough to indicate the extent and the systematic nature of the demographic shifts brought about by Turkey in its pursuit of the Arabization and Turkmenization of the region.

50 "More Than 160,000 Syrian Refugees Return to Regions Liberated from YPG, Daesh," *Daily Sabah Politics*, April 11, 2018, accessed October 2, 2018, https://www.dailysabah.com/politics/2018/04/12/more-than-160000-syrian-refugees-return-to-regions-liberated-from-ypg-daesh.

Voices from Afrin

What follows are original interviews with political and social representatives from Afrin, either done on site or by telephone and/or Skype. They reflect the positions of a broad political spectrum, including the PYD and its allies, the PYD's internal Kurdish opponents, and representatives of religious minorities and their organizations. They were carried out from 2014 to 2018, thereby tracing a historical development.

Hêvî Îbrahîm Mustefa, Prime Minister of the Canton of Afrin | July 30, 2014

In many parts of Syria, there is civil war. What is the situation currently like in the canton of Afrin?
The situation across Syria is very difficult. But we have been fortunate insofar as we have been able to keep the war out of the canton of Afrin so far. While in other parts of Syria there is increasing confessional violence, here the most varied people continue to live in tranquility. We have Sunnis, Shiites, Êzîdî, and Alevi here who live together peacefully. In Afrin, there are Kurds, Arabs, and other minorities who have no problems with each other. They share a certain cohesion, which shows that this could also be the case in other parts of Syria.

You are the only woman among the prime ministers of the autonomous cantons in Rojava. Have the women in Rojava profited from the revolution?
The PYD has always fought for the rights of women. This includes recognizing that women can occupy posts of political responsibility. I am living proof that things really have changed in the Kurdish society.

In the canton of Kobanê, further to the east, there has been heavy fighting between the Kurdish YPG and the Islamic State in recent weeks. You are lucky in that so far you have no border with the Islamic State. Is the situation at the borders of your canton quiet?

It is comparatively quiet. Compared to Kobanê, we are indeed lucky not to be under siege from the Islamic State. All the same, the IS fighters are approaching the borders of our canton from the east and are thus also a threat to us. But so far, we have been able to beat those attacks back. In January, there were also attacks by Jabhat al-Nusra. These groups also try to stir up conflicts among the Kurds. Things are less problematic with the units of the Free Syrian Army present to the south of the canton. In January, Jabhat al-Akrad and the FSA jointly expelled the Islamic State from A'zaz. At this point, we have a sort of coexistence with both the FSA and the government troops stationed in [the Shiite enclave of] Nubl. As long as they don't attack us, we don't attack them.

What's the situation like at the border with Turkey? Is the canton of Afrin also cut off there, or is there a border crossing?

Unfortunately, Turkey has closed the border to all of Rojava, so there is also no legal border crossing between the canton of Afrin and Turkey. While the jihadist groups have access to border crossings, we have to cross the border illegally by night or use the border crossing near A'zaz, which is controlled by the FSA. So our canton also suffers from a Turkish blockade.

How do you see the policy of Europe vis-à-vis Syria and Rojava? What would you want Europe to do?

The European Parliament actually recognized the autonomy of Rojava indirectly two months ago. This was an important step for us. But it would also help us very much if pressure were exerted on Turkey to cease its support for the Islamist opposition and to end the economic blockade against Rojava. Please allow me to use this opportunity to tell Europeans that they should support our revolution here. By fighting the Islamic State terrorists, we also fight for them, and we want a democratic future for Syria. We are the only ones who are still able to put up effective military resistance against this fascist movement. But we don't have a lot of experience with democracy. We need the assistance of Europe to refine our democracy. It is very important that Europe not leave us hanging out to dry and not forget Syria. We are still forced to wage a daily struggle for survival. Nonetheless, we have achieved much, even though we are still at the beginning of our revolution. Our goal is a democratic and autonomous Rojava in a democratic Syria. We need international support to achieve that.

Silêman Ceefer, Foreign Minister of the Canton of Afrin | February 2, 2015

More than a year ago, the three Kurdish cantons proclaimed their autonomy. Have you seen any progress since then with regard to the international recognition of these cantons?

So far, we have not been recognized by the Syrian government or by any other government. Even so, we are increasingly perceived internationally as a partner to enter into contact with. We have also already sent delegations to Europe, and I can see that we are taken increasingly seriously, and that it is now clear that we are one of the few secular and democratic forces in Syria worthy of support.

You are the foreign minister of an entity that is not recognized. How do you fulfil your tasks? How does it feel to be the foreign minister of a canton that is largely cut off from the external world?

This is of course totally different from being the foreign minister of an internationally recognized state. I simply try to do my best to build contacts with states and governments. But you are absolutely right that it is difficult if, in the final analysis, you are not recognized by anyone, have no embassies, and are barely able to travel to foreign countries.

You are an Êzîdî, and your prime minister is an Alevi. The strong presence of the religious minorities in the government here is surprising at first glance.

For us, it is totally normal. The Muslims in Afrin have never been fanatics. Actually, we have always lived together well here. Before I became minister, I was the chairman of an Êzîdî umbrella organization, the Mala Êzîdîya. Everybody here knows that I am an Êzîdî, and I have never had any problems here because of that.

What, in your view, are the biggest problems in the canton?

One of the biggest problems is certainly the isolation. We are severely hampered by the fact that, despite our long border with Turkey, we do not have a single border crossing with this neighbor state of ours and can only leave our area through A'zaz, which is controlled by the Islamic Front, or across the green border into Turkey. Because of Jabhat al-Nusra, it has also become increasingly difficult to get to Aleppo, our traditional urban center. We have become increasingly isolated, and this also has a negative impact on the economy of our cantons.

Fatme Lekto, Minister for Women of the Canton of Afrin | February 2, 2015

How do you try to enforce equality for women in Afrin?
We adopted a female quota of at least 40 percent for all offices and institutions from the beginning. Through our system of codirection, we have women in top positions at all levels. We have employed both women and men in our police force from the start, and the Women's Protection Units are an important part of our army. It is part of our task as a ministry for women to ensure the realization of gender equality in society.

On a social level, changes will be more difficult to realize and slower to effect than on the political plane.
Social changes always take longer to realize. Here in our ministry we can only change the political and legal parameters and encourage women to break free from authoritarian conditions. Thus, we act against polygamy and forced marriages and protect girls who are threatened with violence.

But in a civil war like the one in Syria, women are probably also in danger in very different ways.
Of course, in armed conflicts women are always among the victims. The image of women advocated by the Islamic militias would be horrible even without the civil war. We have the good luck that so far we have largely been able to keep the civil war out of Afrin and have not been overrun by the IS, as in Kobâne. The fact that we could prevent this is due in part to our women who are actively participating in the Women's Protection Units, who do not wait to become victims of the jihadists but are actively defending themselves.

Ebdo Îbrahîm, Minister of Defense of the Canton of Afrin | February 2, 2015

You are the defense minister of a canton that is not internationally recognized, with an army that is not internationally recognized. Nevertheless, at this

The funeral of a YPJ "martyr" from Afrin who was killed in Kobanê in the struggle against the Islamic State.

point, Afrin is one of the safest regions in all of Syria. How did you achieve this?

Our administration places great emphasis on integrating all the groups living here. Almost all the inhabitants of Afrin are Kurds. Therefore, many of the ethnic and religious tensions dominating the other regions of Syria because of the civil war are absent here, and we have succeeded in avoiding the conflicts between the government army and the opposition militias. Moreover, we have repeatedly mediated between the enclave in Nubl and az-Zahrā', which is inhabited by Shiites and held by the government, and the FSA. Actually, the Shiite militias can negotiate with the opposition only through us, and along with Jabhat al-Akrad, the FSA also includes a Kurdish unit with which we cooperate quite well.

During the war against the IS in Kobanê, a general draft for the People's Protection Units (YPG) was introduced in that canton, as well as in the Cizîrê. In these two cantons, the Women's Protection Units (YPJ) are the only remaining volunteer troops.

Up to now we haven't needed a draft. Unlike Kobanê and the Cizîrê, the YPG in Afrin is still a volunteer army. We hope that this will remain the case, but I can't give any guarantees.

Does that mean that you have plans for the introduction of a draft?
No, at the moment there are no such plans. But what happens further down the line certainly depends on the overall military development. Should our security situation worsen dramatically we would certainly also have to think about the introduction of a draft here in Afrin.

In the other cantons, it this sort of draft that triggered widespread criticism by Kurdish opposition groups. This seems to be one of the main critiques leveled by the parties of the so-called Kurdish National Council (ENKS) against the administration of the autonomous cantons founded by the PYD.
We know that. But what can we do when our villages and towns are overrun by IS jihadists? If that happens, everyone will have to participate in the defense. Actually, we don't fight against the IS just for ourselves. Ultimately, by fighting these terrorists we are also defending *your* freedom.

Interview with Three Board Members from the Mala Êzîdîya (House of the Êzîdî) in Afrin | February 3, 2015

How many Êzîdî would you say live in the town Afrin and the villages in the canton?
In 1935, there were around eighty-five Êzîdî villages in Afrin, now only nineteen remain. There are around twenty-five thousand Êzîdî in the entire canton. Over the past twenty years many Êzîdî have gone to Europe, and now many more would like to go, because they are afraid of the attacks of the IS and other jihadist groups. The pressure of the jihadist groups on the Êzîdî has become so great that many of those who now remain also want to leave.

What does the religious infrastructure of the Êzîdî in Afrin look like?
Before the establishment of self-administration in 2012, many people hadn't even revealed that they were Êzîdî. We weren't even allowed to write Kurdish or have symbols of our religion on our gravestones.

But this has now changed?
Yes, now we are free to practice our religion and to found our own institutions. I myself am a sheikh, and according to our social contract we are granted self-administration. Now our little children can learn about our religion. This is the first time in Syrian history that we have religious education at school for the Êzîdî.

Êzîdî cemetery in the village Faqîra, at the edge of the massif called Jebel Seman/ Çiyayê Lêlûn in the south of the canton of Afrin, the location of most Êzîdî villages.

But what does self-administration mean? Is there a separate autonomous region within the larger autonomy? How can one picture the situation?
We have this organization and the Ministry for Religious Affairs within the administration, where we, the Christians, and the Alevi are represented. On March 10, 2013, there was an Êzîdî conference in Afrin where we elected a council. Among the nine members of the council, there are three women, and now we are preparing the next conference. At the previous one, we also founded sub-councils for women, youth, reconciliation, religious affairs, and media.

Do the Êzîdî still follow their traditional marriage rules, that is, a strict endogamy that stipulates marriage only within one's own caste? Is it still the practice that someone from the Murid group is only allowed to marry another Murid, someone from the Sheikh, only a Sheikh, and a Pir, only a Pir?
Yes, this is part of the Êzîdî religion, and it is still the practice.

I have heard a lot of criticism of your organization from other Êzîdî organizations and groups, particularly of the erection of the statue of Zoroaster in

front of the Mala Êzîdîya and the attempt to interpret the Êzîdî religion as
Zoroastrianism. What is your response to that?
I know that people are criticizing this. But if you go back far enough in
history, you will see that Zoroaster was an Êzîdî. When he came along,
there were many flaws in the Êzîdî religion, which he wanted to correct.

In Iraq, for example, in Lefiş, the most sacred Êzîdî site, you won't find any
reference to Zoroaster. There are symbols of Tausî Melek but nothing that
would hint at Zoroaster.
I have often been in Lefiş, and I believe that the opinion of the people there
has more to do with politics than religion. When Zoroaster left Iran for
Afghanistan, his followers there were called Zoroastrians, while here the
name Êzîdî continued to be used. They are one and the same.

Just to be sure that I understand you correctly: Are you saying that the highest
cleric, the Bavê Şêx, and the other dignitaries in Lefiş don't know their reli-
gion well enough to understand that it is actually Zoroastrian?
I have met with the Bavê Şêx eight times. He knows everything about the
religion but not about its historical development. On this point, we just
don't agree. After all the attacks on the Êzîdî, we were increasingly forced
to hide, so many things were lost.

Let's return to the present. Many of the Êzîdî villages are close to regions under
the rule of political Islamic opposition groups. Has this led to attacks on the
Êzîdî by these groups?
The first attack on the Êzîdî was here in Afrin, against the villages of
Qestelê and Basûfanê. That was in 2012, even before the villages near Serê
Kaniyê in the Cizîrê were attacked. At the time, the attackers were units
of the Free Syrian Army, and their maxim was that infidels like us needed
to have our throats cut.

When exactly did these attacks occur, and how many people were killed?
The attacks on Qestelê came in three waves in early 2012, and Basûfanê
was attacked in July 2013. During the attacks on Qestelê, ten people were
killed, and in Basûfanê we lost three fighters.

Have there been attacks on Êzîdî villages since then?

No. There have been several attempts, but the YPG has secured the region with checkpoints and fortifications that have prevented any further attacks on Êzîdî villages since the attack on Basûfanê.

Mesgin Josef, President of the Council of the Syrian Êzîdî (Encûmena Êzidiyên Sûriyê, EÊS) | August 13, 2017
What are the current concrete threats to the Êzîdî in Afrin and other regions in Syria?
Over the past six years, the Syrian Êzîdî have repeatedly been the target of Islamist and terrorist armed groups supported by Turkey, Qatar, and some Syrian oppositionists. These groups have also carried out attacks on Êzîdî villages near Serê Kaniyê. They have killed many of the Êzîdî there, stolen their property, and expelled those they did not kill. We have repeatedly notified the major nations and the Syrian opposition that the Êzîdî in Afrin and in the villages in that area are in extreme danger, both because these villages are often near the Turkish border and because in the eyes of these extremist Islamist terror groups we are infidels.

This situation is also a result of the civil war in Syria. How do you asses the general development of that war?
We, the Council of the Syrian Êzîdî, have renounced armed violence since our founding on March 10, 2012. We also opposed the transforma-tion of the Syrian revolution into an armed revolution, because then it would take an extremist direction and shift away from the correct path all Syrians wanted to take. We Êzîdî are a peaceful people and reject violence.

How is your relation with the Syrian opposition?
Despite our longstanding efforts, the Syrian opposition has always rejected including Êzîdî representatives in the National Coalition for the Syrian Revolution and the Opposition Forces. That said, we also think the PYD's faulty political and military decisions and its rule over the Kurdish areas are a reason for the dire situation of the Êzîdî.

The PYD controls most of the Êzîdî villages in Syria. But in the villages outside the control of the PYD and the YPG/YPJ, the situation clearly seems to be worse. You have publicized the case of the village of Elî Qîno, which is not in a PYD area but between the canton of Afrin and the town A'zaz and controlled

by pro-Turkish militias, and is therefore not protected by the PYD. What happened to the villagers from Elî Qîno?
The village Elî Qîno, near A'zaz, was under the control of the pro-Turkish militias. On June 12, these Islamist rebels gave the people there one hour's notice to leave the village, after which all of the people's property—their olive groves, livestock, and furniture—was confiscated. These people now live as refugees in Afrin. We registered our massive protest against this and called on the international community to strongly condemn these groups.

Your organization, the Council of the Syrian Êzîdî (Encûmena Êzidiyên Sûriyê, EÊS), has its headquarters in Germany. Where are you represented in Syria?
We aren't only headquartered in Germany. We used to have a lot of members in Syria, but they were isolated and faced threats from the PYD. Moreover, we are always at risk of being attacked by armed Islamist groups. Therefore, the majority of our members had to leave their homeland, Syria. Despite these dire circumstances, we still have members in Afrin and al-Hasaka.

What distinguishes your organization from the other Êzîdî organizations in Syria, the Union of the Êzîdî of Syria (Hevbendiya Êzîdiyên Suriyê, HÊS) and the Association of the Êzîdî of West Kurdistan and Syria (Komela Êzdiyên Rojavayê Kurdistanê û Sûriye, KÊRKS)?
The Council of the Syrian Êzîdî was founded on March 10, 2012, to mobilize and centralize the Êzîdî forces. Initially, we formed a preparatory committee consisting of intellectuals, writers, politicians, and well-known personalities. This committee then contacted Êzîdî in the diaspora, in Syria, and around the world to hold a founding conference. The difference between us and the other Êzîdî organizations in Syria, the Union of the Êzîdî of Syria (HÊS) and the Association of the Êzîdî of West Kurdistan and Syria (KÊRKS), is that we refuse to follow the PKK. Those within our organization who tried to push us toward the PKK later split and launched another organization called Hevbendiya Êzîdiyên Suriyê (HÊS). This organization, however, does nothing but praise the PKK and, moreover, is not a political organization but merely a cultural association. These organizations get support and money from the PKK; we don't. They generally try to ruin our reputation, using the PKK media to do so.

In September 2016, you left the Kurdish National Council (ENKS) and the National Coalition (NC), but in May 2017, you rejoined them.

After a year of contact with the Kurdistan Regional Government in Iraq and the Kurdish National Council, we sent five delegates to the ENKS's third conference, in the town of Qamişlo, on June 16, 2015. The conference unanimously agreed that we, as a political organization, represented the Kurdish Êzîdî and should join the Kurdish ENKS. We made the following demands at the conference:

1. In order to build a stable Syrian state, the state and religion must be separate.
2. In the new Syrian constitution, the Êzîdî religion must be recognized as the third largest religion in the country.
3. We demand that we, as Syrian Êzîdî, have a representative in the Syrian national opposition.
4. It is our right to have a representative in the National Council's Kurdish Committee for Foreign Relations.
5. We insist on a representative in the highest organs formed for negotiations.
6. The participants in the Council must regard us as an equal partner and let us participate in political, economic, and military decisions.

The conference agreed to the first three demands, and we withdrew the fourth because it created controversy among the other parties. The last two demands were accepted but never realized. We have been completely marginalized in all political, economic, and military affairs. At first, we retained our member status despite this exclusion and other problems, but we finally withdrew from the ENKS for the following reasons:

1. Many members of the High Negotiations Committee (HNC) of the Syrian opposition attacked the Kurdish people with racist statements and descriptions, and yet the ENKS remained a member in that body.
2. The ENKS did nothing to oppose the agreement of the donors' conference in London.[1]

---

1   The results of the February 2016 Supporting Syria and the Region conference organized by Norway, the United Kingdom, Germany, and Kuwait were seen as support for Turkey, whose government has traditionally been hostile to the Êzîdî, while some member organizations of the Muslim-dominated ENKS are on relatively good terms with Turkey.

3. The Islamization of the Syrian revolution and the deliberate deviation of the Syrian revolution from its path was another reason we resigned.

4. The Kurdish National Council systematically ignored and marginalized the Council of the Syrian Êzîdî. The Kurdistan Regional Government was notified of this and did nothing.

5. The Êzîdî were excluded from all negotiations in Geneva and in no way represented in any of them.

The ENKS often participated in negotiations without the Êzîdî, did not share any of the financial support it got from the Kurdistan Regional Government in Iraq with us, and did not even notify us of meetings with that government. So we resigned both from the Kurdish National Council and the National Coalition for Syrian Revolutionary and Opposition Forces.

And why have you rejoined?
After we withdrew from both opposition platforms, the ENKS and the NC, very many independent Kurdish and Arab politicians, intellectuals, writers, and well-known personalities contacted us. Then later, the Kurdistan Regional Government also contacted us and asked us to rejoin. We wrote a letter to the ENKS on February 8, 2017, which included a very important sentence, specifically: "We are willing to return to the ENKS if the reasons for our resignation cease and we receive assurances that the these things will not happen again in the future." On May 4, 2017, we received a written response to this letter from the ENKS, signed by Dr. Kamiran Haj Abdo, who is the chairman of the Kurdish Democratic Unity Party and a member of the executive committee of the ENKS, saying that at a ENKS meeting on March 17, 2017, all members unanimously voted for the readmission of the Council of the Syrian Êzîdî. It is our hope and desire that these promises will be kept on all levels, and that we will be treated as equal partners.

Kamal Sido, Middle East Consultant of the Society for Threatened Peoples | March 11, 2018
You come from Afrin, and in 2015 you had a long sojourn there. How did you find the mood of the population at the time, and what have you heard since from your relatives and acquaintances in Afrin?

The last time I was in Afrin was in 2015, but since then I have been in contact with the people there on a daily basis. Back then, the situation was stable, but the area struck me as a large prison, because the people could neither enter nor leave. At the time, there were no military attacks by Islamists or Turkey but some sort of an armistice, so I was able to travel to Afrin via A'zaz. I was afraid at the time, but I managed to make it.

I took the very same road to Afrin in 2015. But unfortunately, after 2015, this road was closed.
Yes, unfortunately Afrin has become even more isolated since then. But it was precarious even in 2015. At the time, I didn't post anything on the social media, because I knew that I would have to take the same border crossing back. Therefore, I didn't give any interviews on the radio or anywhere else.

What was your impression of the people at the time? You and I were there at almost the same time after all, and my impression was that the people in Afrin had it pretty good compared to other regions in Syria.
Yes, by and large the people were doing pretty well then. I visited a school, and the children were very proud to finally be able to learn Kurdish. Not all the parents were enthusiastic, but the children were. No one was more enthusiastic than me, telling the children about the old days when we had to hide Kurdish books. Of course, there was also dissatisfaction with the administration. Members of the opposition parties in particular complained about the PYD. But ordinary people were, for the most part, relatively content with the situation. Generally feeling secure was part of this. One could travel everywhere. There were no holdups or robberies. My mother and sister lived alone at their home with no problem at all. They always felt completely safe.

You are the Middle East consultant of the Society for Threatened Peoples and have dealt with the minorities in the region for many years. At the moment, the "double minorities" are probably particularly vulnerable—those who are not only Kurds but also members of a religious minority who the militias allied with Turkey regard as heretics, or, in the case of the Êzîdî, even as devil worshippers. What do they have to fear?
At the time, I met my first Armenian in Afrin. I had been trying to find him for a long time and finally managed to meet him on the next to last

day before my departure. I spoke with him extensively, because we were producing a documentary for the occasion of the hundredth anniversary of the 1915 genocide. I spoke with the Êzîdî, as well as with the Büd, whose traditional role is similar to the Roma in Europe. Those minorities felt safe, as did those expelled from other regions, whose situation was also okay. For me, it was important that the minorities felt well and secure, which seemed to be the case. Part of this is that, for a number of reasons, the Muslims in Afrin are very tolerant. Many Muslim Kurds in Afrin are of Alevi or Êzîdî descent and have not forgotten this. I heard many stories, including that this Armenian was, for example, afraid to send his son to purchase goods in Aleppo, lest the people there realize that he was an Armenian. The Alevi were also afraid to move into territory controlled by the Sunni Arab militias. Actually, as early as 2015, people from Mabeta were no longer able to travel to Aleppo. Merely having Mabeta stamped on your ID raised the risk of being suspected of being an Alevi. Even the people in the village my wife comes from, who are Sunni, but nonetheless live in Mabeta, could no longer go to Aleppo, because they would have been suspected of being Alevi. And the Êzîdî tried to learn to pray like the Muslims, in order to be able to pose as Muslims should the need arise. All of this to say that the religious minorities were already afraid in 2015.

What will it mean if Turkey actually conquers Afrin?
The fact is that Turkey is fighting alongside the very militias that the religious minorities already feared in 2015. For these minorities, the conquest of Afrin by Turkey would be disastrous.

You are not a PKK sympathizer but a liberal and, in fact, a member of the German Free Democratic Party, the FDP. Have you met with the members of the political opposition who have repeatedly criticized the authoritarianism of the PYD?
Of course, and that led to a lot of criticism from the members of the Kurdish National Council (ENKS). But it was political criticism that was not related to the actual local situation. It is well-known that the PYD and the PDK, the first close to the PKK and the second to Barzani's PDK, are always quarrelling. They just can't seem to cooperate. I have visited members of the National Council, including a politician who is now in jail. They criticize the PYD system, but these two factions will always criticize each other,

with absolutely no regard for what the other side is actually doing at any given point. The problem is that the PYD opposes Turkey and the Islamists, and that's exactly who the ENKS works with, the opposition supported by Turkey. That means reconciliation between the two will not be possible if neither switches sides.

How do you assess the current relationship between the PYD and the ENKS? Has the attack by Turkey intensified the internal Kurdish tensions or has it defused them?

Turkey's attack on Afrin has increased the internal Kurdish tensions, because the ENKS has not broken with the Syrian opposition, even though many Kurds had expected that it would once the Turkish attacks began. Instead, the ENKS acts as if nothing has happened and continues to hold meetings with the pro-Turkish Syrian opposition.

You live in Germany and have witnessed the German and the European reaction to the Turkish attack on Afrin. Why haven't the German federal government or the EU Commission criticized Turkey's actions?

The Kurds had expected that Germany, the EU, and the U.S. would react more critically and would condemn Turkey's attack on the Kurds. For us, the Society for Threatened Peoples, this is a war of aggression in violation of international law. Obviously, the Kurds feel forsaken. We have fought against the Islamic State. Many Kurds say, "We have shared values, like women's rights and so on, but now we are left in the lurch." Of course, the PYD's human rights violations don't make it particularly sympathetic, even if these transgressions are not systematic. I have visited many prisons in Rojava. There are human rights violations, which we criticize, but compared to the situation as a whole, they are not systematic. We have to give our critical support to this project. We must also criticize all false arrests and human rights violations, but the Kurds would certainly want us to support this project.

Salih Muslim, the Movement for a Democratic Society (TEV-DEM) Spokesperson for Foreign Affairs, Co-Chair of the PYD until 2017 | March 13, 2018

During Turkey's attack on Afrin, you were arrested in Prague on a Turkish warrant. This happened although you had been in Turkey several times in 2014 and were even received by officials during the attacks of the so-called

Islamic State on Kobanê. What changed? Why do you think Turkey wants you arrested now?

Inviting me to Turkey was a game to induce us to adopt Turkey's positions and help it achieve its goals, as well as to conceal its support for the Islamic State. Since then, all of this has become clear. We publicly exposed their dirty tricks and their relationship with the Islamic State and other terrorist organizations. So now they are trying to silence us and to connect us with the PKK and to all sorts of things that have happened in Turkey.

What do you have to say about reactions in Europe to this?

I'm not a Turkish citizen, and I trust the courts of the European Union.

How do you evaluate the reactions of the EU and its member states to the Turkish attacks?

The governments of the EU states are very focused on their own interests and are very pragmatic. We hope that the humanity, the humane values, and the will and wishes of the European peoples will come to play a bigger role in the implementation of the EU rules than has previously been the case and that the principles of democracy will become more important when dealing with the Kurdish question and the attack on Afrin.

Many Europeans have a lot of sympathy for the Kurds and don't understand why their governments are doing nothing to oppose the war against Afrin. I too am often asked what citizens in Europe can do for you. What would you respond to people who, as ordinary citizens, want to do something against an impending massacre in Afrin?

We hope to continue to work with Kurds in Europe on democratic initiatives in order to exert more pressure on the governments and EU institutions, particularly those bodies that deal with EU policy on the Kurdish question and the Middle East.

What Next?

On March 18, 2018, the city of Afrin fell into the hands of the Turkish army and its Islamist allies. Most of the civilians were evacuated from the town. Thereafter, Kurdish units could hold their ground only in rural retreat areas in the central hilly regions of the canton and in the far east on the high plateau of the Ǧabal Simʿān (Kurdish: Çiyayê Lêlûn). While the fighters in the central hills have mostly gone underground to prepare for a guerilla struggle, the last—primarily Êzîdî—villages on the Çiyayê Lêlûn around Fatirtin, Bircilqasê, and Meyasê are still held by the YPG, and the same is true of a large part of the area around Tal Rifaat captured by the YPG in 2016.

In the case of the city of Afrin, we can see the crucial difference between leftist and rightist violence. The YPG apparently decided to respect civilian lives, rather than defending the city to the last breath. Realizing it could not defend the city, it chose not to fight to the point of complete annihilation as the IS did in Raqqa and Mosul. There will certainly come a point for discussing the political and military mistakes of the YPG and the PYD, but with their final decision to refrain from risking a heroic but senseless doom and gloom scenario, they did what was in their power to protect civilian lives. In my view, this deserves respect. But it also means that the international community now bears responsibility for the civilians from Afrin!

A book can never be completely up-to-date. It can only highlight the background and context and, in our case, focus attention on all the things that are being destroyed, on the world that is being annihilated, on the people who are being killed and turned into refugees. Whether the last

Kurdish units will be defeated before this book comes out or will be able to continue resisting remains to be seen, but the fact that the struggle over Afrin has entered its final phase with the fall of the city of Afrin can hardly be denied.

So far, however, the YPG and the YPJ have not capitulated. When the body of this book was completed in spring 2018, not only did the YPG still hold retreat areas on the high plateau of the Ǧabal Simʿān, but the battle for the rest of Afrin had not been entirely given up. On the contrary, on March 18, several speakers from the canton and the YPG announced the latter's intention to continue the fight a guerilla struggle and to return to Afrin. Of course, only the future will tell whether and to what degree the Kurdish fighters will be able to do this, and the same is true for the question of whether any of the retreat areas can ultimately be held and, if so, which ones.

Be that as it may, by the summer of 2018, the YPG had intensified its activities in Afrin. The number of targeted killings of Turkish soldiers and Syrian Islamist militiamen has clearly risen since June 2018. Moreover, with the Efrîn Falcons (Teyrêbazên Efrînê), a new underground organization emerged in June 2018 that has been contributing to the destabilization of the Turkish Islamist rule in Afrin with bomb attacks. Whether the Efrîn Falcons are actually a subunit of the YPG is as of yet unclear. In a statement of June 29, the Falcons claimed to be politically independent and to have formed to fight the occupiers using their own forces because of the failure of the international community, the local Kurdish forces, and the Kurdish parties. In the part of Rojava that remains under YPG control the Efrîn Falcons are not very popular, as there are some indications that they might have connections with the Syrian Regime.

Regardless of how this new phase of the war develops, this book is not meant as a melancholy swansong or a mere epitaph for the "Mountain of the Kurds" but as a contribution to the struggle for liberation, democracy, and equality—a contribution to the goal of giving all human beings, including the inhabitants of the region of Afrin, the possibility to lead a peaceful, free, and happy life. The fall of Afrin has certainly not ended this struggle, because it is not the struggle of a particular militia or party but a political struggle for basic human rights for all inhabitants of the region.

Though many fighters and civilians were killed in the battle for the mountain of the Kurds, many have remained in the region and are now suffering under the Turkish occupation regime. Moreover, around two

The urban middle classes of the town would like to have U.S. coffee chains in the region, but for the time being they have to make do with imitations.

hundred thousand displaced persons urgently need both humanitarian aid and a political solution. Even though the "Mountain of the Kurds" is now in the hands of the Turkish army led by the tyrannical Commander in Chief Erdoğan and his jihadist allies, all of us still have a responsibility to fight for the right all of these people to return to their homes and for the expulsion of the occupying tyrants.

Neither the international community, which must address, resist, and reverse the illegal expulsion of the population, the settlement of people from the outside, and the destruction of cultural goods and olive gardens, nor the progressive political movements throughout the world can possibly accept the expulsion of these people. Both the law of war and international law demand that the expelled civilians be permitted to safely return to their homes.

The fact that the military units designated as "terrorists" by the Turkish side have long since withdrawn from the region should have pulled the rug out from under the Turkish government's justification for its further military presence in the region, given that it claims to be merely acting against "terrorists"—and there is even less justification for replacing the original population of the region with people primarily introduced to give the Turkish regime permanent control over the region.

If Turkey and its allies are permitted to establish any form of a "Turkish Republic of North Syria," this will create a new center of conflict that will fester for many years to come. Hundreds of thousands of those expelled from Afrin would then have to continue their flight to Europe.

Thanks to the restrictive Turkish press policy we know little about what is going on inside Afrin. However, what we do know tells us a lot. Displaced Kurds are not allowed to return, while Arabs and Turkmens are resettled in the region. Even more than Muslim Kurds, however, religious minorities suffer under the occupation by Turkey and its allies. The sacred sites of the Alevis and Yazidis have been desecrated and destroyed. In May 2018, the Yazidi cemetery in Gundê Feqîra and the Shrine of Sheikh Jened were targeted. In November 2018, the one-hundred-year-old Ziyaret of Av Girê was desecrated and partly destroyed by the pro-Turkish Ahrar al-Sharqiya militia. Members of these minority groups have been abducted, and there are reports of forced conversions to Sunni Islam. Christians fled to Kobanê, which is still under YPG control, and reopened a church there in September.

Nonetheless, the occupation isn't really working as planned from a Turkish perspective. In November 2018, heavy fighting erupted between different pro-Turkish militias in Afrin, with about a dozen casualties on each side. The region is de facto annexed to and ruled by the neighboring Turkish governorates. Turkey has opened post offices and schools with Turkish curricula that serve the new inhabitants of the region, but many of its original inhabitants are still living in tents in the canton of Shahba, a small piece of isolated land squeezed between the regime and the pro-Turkish militias.

With the withdrawal of the YPG and the YPJ and the expulsion of about two hundred thousand civilians from the region, the international community, which allowed this war to happen, bears responsibility for the fate of these civilians. The battle for the Mountain of the Kurds is far from over!

Acronym Key

AKP   Justice and Development Party (Adalet ve Kalkınma Partisi): President Erdorğan's right-wing ruling party in Turkey.

CHP   Republican People's Party (Cumhuriyet Halk Partisi): Kemalist party with nationalist and authoritarian social democratic elements.

EÊS   Council of the Êzîdî of Syria (Encûmena Êzdiyên Sûriyê): Êzîdî organization in Syria.

ENKS   Kurdish National Council in Syria (Encûmena Niştimanî ya Kurdî li Sûriyeyê): umbrella organization of Kurdish parties in Syria connected with the Kurdish regional government in Iraq, does not include the PYD.

HDP   Peoples' Democratic Party (Halkların Demokratik Partisi): left-wing pro-Kurdish political party in Turkey.

HÊS   Union of the Êzîdî of Syria (Hevbendiya Êzîdiyên Suriyê): Êzîdî organization in Syria.

HPG   People's Defense Forces (Hêzên Parestina Gel): armed wing of the Kurdistan Workers' Party, PKK.

KÊRKS   Association of the Êzîdî of West Kurdistan and Syria (Komela Êzdiyên Rojavayê Kurdistanê û Sûriye): Êzîdî organization in Syria.

MHP   Nationalist Movement Party (Milliyetçi Hareket Partisi): extreme right-wing nationalist political party in Turkey.

PDK   Kurdistan Democratic Party (Partiya Demokrata Kurdistanê): Kurdish conservative nationalist party led by the Barzani family in the Kurdish region of Iraq, mainly based in Erbil and Dohuk.

PDKS   Democratic Party of Kurdistan in Syria (Partiya Demokrata Kurdistan a Sûriye): the PDK's Syrian sister party.

PKK   Kurdistan Workers' Party (Partiya Karkerên Kurdistanê): militant Kurdish political party led by Abdullah Öcalan, sister organization of the PYD.

PUK   Patriotic Union of Kurdistan (Yekêtiy Nîştimaniy Kurdistan): social democratic and liberal party in the Kurdish region of Iraq, established by Jalal Talabani in 1975, mainly based in Suleymania.

PYD   Democratic Union Party (Partiya Yekîtîya Demokrat): Syrian Kurdish political party established by members of the PKK in Syria.

SDF   Syrian Democratic Forces (Hêzên Sûriya Demokratîk): umbrella organization of the YPG and the YPJ with Arab, Christian-Aramaic, and Turkmen allies.

TEV-DEM Movement for a Democratic Society (Tevgera Civaka Demokratîk): coalition of parties and civil society groups governing the de facto autonomous region of the Democratic Federation of Northern Syria (DFNS).

YBŞ   Resistance Units of Şingal (Yekîneyên Berxwedana Şengalê): Êzîdî armed forces sympathetic with the PKK in Sinjar (Şingal).

YJÊ   Women's Units of Êzidxan (Yekineyen Jinên Êzidxan): female armed forces of the Êzîdî who are sympathetic with the PKK and who coordinate with the YBŞ.

YPG   People's Protection Units (Yekîneyên Parastina Gel): Kurdish armed forces established by the PYD.

YPJ   Women's Protection Units (Yekîneyên Parastina Jin): female Kurdish armed forces who fight alongside the YPG.

Bibliography

Acikiyildiz, Birgül. *The Yezidis: The History of a Community, Culture and Religion*. London, I.B. Tauris, 2010.

Ali, Muhammed Abdo. *Jabal al-Ākrād (Afrīn): Dirasat tārihiyah ijtimāiyah tawthiqiyah*. Suleymania, IQ: 2009.

Allison, Christine. "'Unbelievable Slowness of Mind': Yezidi Studies, from Nineteenth to Twenty-First Century." *Journal of Kurdish Studies* 6, (2008): 1–23.

Allsopp, Harriet. *The Kurds of Syria: Political Parties and Identities in the Middle East*. London: I.B. Tauris, 2014.

Basch-Harod, Heidi. "The Kurdish Women in Turkey: Nation Building and the Struggle for Gender Parity." In *Kurdish Awakening: Nation Building in a Fragmented Homeland*. Edited by Ofra Bengio, 175–90. Austin: University of Texas Press, 2014.

Bidlissī, Sharaf Khan. *Chèref-Nâmeh ou fastes de la nation Kourde*. 4 vols. Translated by F.B. Charmoy. St. Petersburg: Commissionnaires de l'Académie impériale des sciences, 1868–1875.

Bidwell, Robin. *Dictionary of Modern Arab History: An A to Z of Over 2,000 Entries from 1798 to the Present Day*. London: Routledge, 2010.

Bittner, Maximilian. *Die heiligen Bücher der Jesiden oder Teufelsanbeter*. Vienna: Alfred Hölder Verlag, 1913.

Çetin, Ihsan. *Midyat'ta etnik gruplar: Kürtler, Mhalmiler (Araplar), Süryaniler, Yezidiler, Türkler, Becırmaniler (Seyyidler)*. Istanbul: Yaba Yayınları, 2007.

Cheterian, Vicken. *Open Wounds: Armenians, Turks and a Century of Genocide*. New York: Oxford University Press, 2015.

Fartacek, Gerhard. *Pilgerstätten in der syrischen Peripherie: Eine ethnologische Studie zur kognitiven Konstruktion sakraler Plätze und deren Praxisrelevanz*. Vienna: Verlag der Österreichischen Akademie der Wissenschaften, 2003.

Flach, Anja, Ercan Ayboğa, and Michael Knapp. *Revolution in Rojava: Frauenbewegung und Kommunalismus zwischen Krieg und Embargo*. Hamburg: VSA: Verag, 2015. [For a revised and updated translation, see Knapp et al. below.]

Galip, Özlem Belçim. *Imagining Kurdistan: Identity, Culture and Society*. London: I.B. Taurus & Co., 2015.

George, Alan. *Syria: Neither Bread nor Freedom*. London: Zed Books, 2003.

Güleryüz, Naim. *The Synagogues of Turkey: The Synagogues of Thrace and Anatolia*. Istanbul: Gozlem Gazetecilik Basin ve Yayin A.S. 2008.

Gunter, Michael M. *Out of Nowhere: The Kurds of Syria in Peace and War*. London: Oxford University Press, 2014.

Halhalli, Bekir. "Kurdish Political Parties in Syria: Past Struggles and Future Expectations." In *Comparative Kurdish Politics in the Middle East: Actors, Ideas, and Interests*. Edited by Emel Tugdar and Serhun Al, 27–53. New York: Palgrave Macmillan 2018.

Holt, P.M. *The Age of the Crusades: The Near East from the Eleventh Century to 1517*. London: Routledge, 2013.

Kaya, Zeynep, and Robert Lowe. "The Curious Question of the PYD-PKK Relationship." In *The Kurdish Question Revisited*. Edited by Gareth Stansfield and Mohammed Shareef, 275–87. London: Oxford University Press, 2017.

Khouri, Philip Shukri. *Syria and the French Mandate: The Politics of Arab Nationalism, 1920–1945*. Princeton, NJ: Princeton University Press, 1987.

Knapp, Michael, Anja Flach, and Ercan Ayboğa. *Revolution in Rojava: Democratic Autonomy and Women's Liberation in Syrian Kurdistan*. London: Pluto Press, 2016. [A revised and updated translation of Flach et al. above.]

Kondo, Osamu, and Hajime Ishida. "Ontogenetic Variation in the Dederiyeh Neandertal Infants: Postcranial Evidence." In *Patterns of Growth and Development in the Genus Homo*. Edited by Jennifer L. Thompson, Gail E. Krovitz, and Andrew J. Nelson, 386–411. Cambridge: Cambridge University Press, 2003.

Kreyenbroek, Philip G. "Die Eziden, die Ahl-e Haqq und die Religion des Zarathustra." In *Im Transformationsprozess: Die Eziden und das Ezidentum gestern, heute, morgen: Beiträge der zweiten internationalen GEA-Konferenz vom 04. bis 05.10.2014 in Bielefeld*. Edited by Gesellschaft Ezidischer AkademikerInnen, 27–33. Berlin: VWB-Verlag, 2016.

Krois, Peter. *Kultur und literarische Übersetzung—eine Wechselbeziehung. Österreichische und syrisch-arabische Kontextualisierung von Kurzgeschichten Zakariyyā Tāmirs*. Berlin: Lit Verlag, 2012.

Kumral, Mehmet Akif. *Rethinking Turkey-Iraq Relations: The Dilemma of Partial Cooperation*. New York: Palgrave Macmillan, 2016.

Lange, Katharina. "Peripheral Experiences: Everyday Life in Kurd Dagh (Northern Syria) During the Allied Occupation in the Second World War." In *The World in World Wars: Perspectives, Experiences and Perceptions from Asia and Africa*. Edited by Heike Liebau, Katrin Bromber, Katharina Lange, Dyala Hamzah, and Ravi Ahuja, 401–28. Leiden, NL: Brill, 2010.

Lescot, Roger. *Enquête sur les Yézidis de Syrie et du Djebel Sindjar*. Beirut: Institut français de Damas, 1938.

———. "Le Kurd Dagh et le Mouvement Mouroud." *Studio Kurdica* (1988): 101–25.

Maisel, Sebastian: *Yezidis in Syria: Identity Building among a Double Minority*. Lanham, MD: Lexington Books, 2017.

Mansel, Philip. *Aleppo: The Rise and Fall of Syria's Great Merchant City*. London: I.B. Taurus & Co., 2016.

Marcus, Aliza. *Blood and Belief: The PKK and the Kurdish Fight for Independence*. New York: New York University Press, 2007.

Masters, Bruce. "Semi-Autonomous Forces in the Arab Provinces." In *The Cambridge History of Turkey, Vol.3: The Late Ottoman Empire 1603–1839*. Edited by Suraiyan Faroqhi, 186–206. Cambridge: Cambridge University Press, 2006.

Matras, Yaron. *A Grammar of Domari*. Berlin: Walter de Gruyter GMBH & Co., 2012.

———. "Grammatical Borrowing in Domari." In *Grammatical Borrowing in Cross-Linguistic Perspective*. Edited by Yaron Matras and Jeanette Sakel, 152–64. Berlin: Walter de Gruyter GMBH & Co., 2007.

Migliorino, Nicola. *(Re)Constructing Armenia in Lebanon and Syria: Ethno-Cultural Diversity and the State in the Aftermath of a Refugee Crisis*. New York: Berghahn Books, 2008.

Oron, Yitzkhak, ed. *Middle East Record 1961*. Vol. 2. Jerusalem: Israel Program for Scientific Translations, 1961.

Pinto, Paulo. "Kurdish Sufi Spaces of Rural-Urban: Connection in Northern Syria." *Études Rurales* 186 (2010).

Schmidinger, Thomas. "Alevitische 'Identitäten'—Eine heterodoxe Religionsgemeinschaft zwischen Islam und Pantheismus, türkischem, kurdischem und Zaza-Nationalismus." In *Kurdistan im Wandel Konflikte, Staatlichkeit, Gesellschaft und Religion zwischen Nahem Osten und Diaspora*. Edited by Thomas Schmidinger, 53–62. Vienna: Peter Lang Verlag, 2011.

———. *Krieg und Revolution in Syrisch-Kurdistan: Analysen und Stimmen aus Rojava*. Vienna: Mandelbaum Verlag, 2014 [4th edition 2017] [For a revised and updated translation, see *Rojava: Revolution, War, and the Future of Syria's Kurds* below.].

———. "Militärische Expansion mit US-Unterstützung: Aktuelle Entwicklungen in Syrisch-Kurdistan." In *Wiener Jahrbuch für Kurdische Studien 5: Sprache—Migration—Zusammenhalt: Kurdisch und seine Diaspora*. Edited by Katharina Brizíc, Agnes Grond, Christoph Osztovics, Thomas Schmidinger, and Maria Anna Six-Hohenbalken, 234–40. Vienna: Praesens Verlag, 2017.

———. *Rojava*. Vienna: Mandelbaum Verlag, 2016.

———. *Rojava: Revolution, War, and the Future of Syria's Kurds*. London: Pluto Press, 2018. [A revised and updated translation of *Krieg und Revolution in Syrisch-Kurdistan* above.]

———. "Westarmenien in Kurdistan: Überleben und Exil armenischer Gemeinden in Kurdistan hundert Jahre nach dem Genozid." *Wiener Jahrbuch für Kurdische Studien 3: 100 Jahre Völkermord an ArmenierInnen und die KurdInnen: Komplexe Vergangenheit und Nachwirken in die Gegenwart*. Edited by Ferdinand Hennerbichler, Chrstoph Osztovics, Maria Anna Six-Hohenbalken, Thomas Schmidinger, 137–84. Vienna: Praesens Verlag, 2015.

Sinclair, T.A. *Eastern Turkey: An Architectural and Archaeological Survey*. Vol. 6. London: Pindar Press 1990.

Spät, Eszter. *The Yezidis*. London: Saqi, 2005.

Tachjian, Vahé. *Le France en Cilicie et en Haute-Mésopotamie: Aux confins de la Turquie, de la Syrie et de l'Iraq (1919–1933)*. Paris: Éditions Karthala, 2004.

Tejel, Jordi. *Syria's Kurds: History, Politics and Society*. London: Routledge, 2009.

Vanly, Ismet Chérif. "The Kurds in Syria and Lebanon." In *The Kurds: A Contemporary Overview*. Edited by Philip G. Kreyenbroek, 112–34. London: Routledge, 1992.

Vorhoff, Karin. *Zwischen Glaube, Nation und neuer Gemeinschaft: Alevitische Identität in der Türkei der Gegenwart*. Berlin: Klaus Schwartz Verlag, 1995.

Yildiz, Kerim. *The Kurds in Syria: The Forgotten People*. London: Pluto Press, 2005.

Index

Page numbers in *italic* refer to illustrations. "Passim" (literally "scattered") indicates intermittent discussion of a topic over a cluster of pages.

Abdalla, Nesrîn, 48
Abdo, Kamiran Haj, 124
Adalet ve Kalkınma Partisi (AKP), 77, 100, 133
Afghanistan, 99, 100
Afrin Council, 110, 111
agriculture, 2–3, 57, 60; origins, 23
Ahfad al-Rasul Brigade, 110
Ahrar ash-Sham, 65, 66, 74, 75, 81n6
AKP. *See* Adalet ve Kalkınma Partisi (AKP)
Alawi and Alawites, 14, 16, 21, 32
Aleppo, 1–7 passim, 19, 29–32 passim, 61, 69, 74–76, 126; accessibility, 116; ancient trade routes, 23; crusader attacks on, 26; immigration from Afrin, 94–95; Jews, 20, 21; refugees from, 62; Saladin conquest, 27; U.S. and, 80; YPG withdrawal from, 94
Alevi and Alevism, 1, 15–17, 21, 50, 100, 115, 119
Alexander the Great, 25
Ali, Mihyedîn Şêx, 53
Ali Canpolat, 29
Al-Nusra Front. *See* Jabhat al-Nusra
al-Qaeda, 65, 74
Ammo, Ismail, 52–53

Anatolia, 38
Antakya, Turkey, 20–21, 34
Antioch, 17, 20, 25, 26
Aoun, Michel, 18
Aouni, Hassan, 33
Apo, Abdelrehman, 53, 91
Arabic, 5, 6, 21, 37, 43, 61
Arabization, xv, 37, 78, 102–5 passim, 112
Arak, 19, 57
archaeological sites, 8, 22–26 passim
Armenian Secret Army for the Liberation of Armenia (ASALA), 39
Armenians, 4, 18–19, 31, 57, 125–26; genocide and refugees, 32–33, 126
arms exports, German, 98–99
Assad, Bashar al-, 44, 60
Assad, Hafiz al-, 21, 38, 44
Assad family, 21, 44
Association of the Êzîdî of West Kurdistan and Syria (Komela Êzdiyên Rojavayê Kurdistanê û Sûriye). *See* Komela Êzdiyên Rojavayê Kurdistanê û Sûriye (KÊRKS)
Austria, 45n55, 84, 89, 99
Ayaz, Abdullah, 112

Ayyubids, 27
Azadî Battalion, 72–73, 74
Azadî Brigade, 92n25
az-Zahrā', 21, 60, 62, 66, 68, 95, 109, 117

Ba'ath Party, 36–37
Barzani, Masoud, 90, 92, 111
Barzani family, 8n2, 39n44, 90
Biro, Ibrehîm, 110–11
Bittner, Maximilian: *The Holy Books of the Êzîdî or Devil Worshippers*, 11
Bookchin, Murray, 49, 51
border controls, 66–67, 114–16 passim; walls, 67, 69, 73, 84
British in Syria, 31, 34, 35
Büd, 5–6, 93, 126

Canpolat, Ali. *See* Ali Canpolat
Canpolat Beğ, 28–29
Cavuşoğlu, Mevlüt, 88–89
Ceefer, Silêman, 115–16
cemetery desecration, 109
chemical weapons, 94
CHP. *See* Cumhuriyet Halk Partisi (CHP)
Christians, 14, 17–20, 103, 119; Antioch, 25–26; archaeological sites, 26; crusaders, 7, 26, 27; political parties, 55
Cindirês (city), 6, 18–20 passim, 95
Cockburn, Patrick, 102–3n40
Communist Party of Syria, 35, 36
conscription. *See* military draft
cooperatives, 59–60
Council of the Syrian Êzîdî. *See* Encûmena Êzidiyên Sûrî (EÊS)
council systems, 50–52 passim
Cumaa, Mustafa, 72–73
Cumhuriyet Halk Partisi (CHP), 77, 133
Cyrrhus, 26

Damascus, 27, 39, 42, 81
dams, 38, 43, 105
Dashnaks, 33
De Gaulle, Charles, 35

democracy, xi, xiii, 35, 47, 51, 52, 114, 128
"Democratic Federation of North Syria" (name), 53
Democratic Nation list. *See* Lîsta Netewa Demokratîk (LND)
Democratic Party of the Kurds in Syria. *See* Partiya Dêmokrat a Kurd li Sûriyê (PDKS)
Democratic Union Party. *See* Partiya Yekítîya Demokrat (PYD)
demonstrations, 42, 45n55, 46, 47; Germany, 98
Descendants of Saladin Brigade, 72, 79, 92n25
Desteya Bilind a Kurd. *See* Supreme Kurdish Committee
Deutsch Rotes Kreuz (German Red Cross), 87
displaced people. *See* refugees
draft, military. *See* military draft
dress codes, Islamist, xiv, 111
Druze, 1, 14, 28
Dūmī, 5, 41

East Ghouta, xv, 81, 111
economy, 57–60. *See also* agriculture
education, 60–62, 125
Efrîn Falcons, 130
Egypt, 36, 43
elections, 35, 36, 42, 55, 56
electricity, 38, 58
Elî Qîno, 13, 73, 121–22
Elîko, Fûad, 110–11
Encûmena Êzidiyên Sûriyê (EÊS), 15, 121, 122, 133
Encûmena Niştimanî ya Kurdî li Sûriyeyê (ENKS). See Kurdish National Council (ENKS)
Enîya Kurdan. *See* Jabhat al-Akrad (Enîya Kurdan)
Erbil, 50, 103, 134
Erdoğan, Emine, 101
Erdoğan, Recep Tayyip, xiv, 77–80 passim, 84–110 passim, 131
European Parliament, 88, 114

European Union (EU), xv, 44, 78, 88, 99–100, 128
Êzîdî, 9–15, 28, 50, 66, 73, 93, 103, 107–10 passim, 115–29 passim

Feisal I, King, 31
feudalism, 30, 31
Foundation for Political, Economic and Social Research (Turkey). *See* Siyaset, Ekonomi ve Toplum Araştırmaları Vakfı (SETA)
Free Syrian Army (FSA), 65–66, 68, 74, 85, 97, 114, 117, 120
French protectorate of Syria, 21, 31–35

Gabriel, Sigmar, 98
GAP. *See* Güneydoğu Anadolu Projesi (GAP)
Germany, xiv–xv, 45n55, 88, 89, 91, 122, 123n1; arms exports, 98–99; Free Democratic Party (FDP), 126; Red Cross, 87; Turkish-Islamic Union of the Institution for Religion, 84
Gesellschaft für bedrohte Völker (GfbV). *See* Society for Threatened Peoples (Germany)
Ghalib, Ali, 33
Ghorbat. *See* Büd
grave desecration, 109
Great Britain. *See* United Kingdom
Güneydoğu Anadolu Projesi (GAP), 38

Haftaro family, 59
Hai'at Tahrir ash-Sham, 13, 80, 81n6, 94n27
Hajo, Siamend, 91
Halkların Demokratik Partisi (HDP), 45n55, 48, 78, 84, 133
Hamidiye regiments, 30–31
Hanānū, Ibrāhīm, 32, 33
Harakat Nur ad-Din az-Zanki, 66, 74, 75
Hashemites, 31, 32

Hatay State. *See* Republic of Hatay
hawala. *See* remittances, international (hawala)
Hayat Tahrir al-Sham, 80, 81n6, 94n27
HDP. *See* Halkların Demokratik Partisi (HDP)
Hevbendiya Êzîdiyên Suriyê (HÊS), 15, 122, 133
Hevbendiya Niştimanî a Kurdî li Sûriyê. *See* Kurdish National Alliance in Syria
Hêzên Hevbendiya Gel (HPG), 48, 133
Hittites, 23
The Holy Books of the Êzîdî or Devil Worshippers (Bittner), 11
hospital bombings, 106
HPG. *See* Hêzên Parastina Gel (HPG)
Hungary, 99
Hurrians, 23, 24
Hussein, Saddam, 103
hydroelectric projects, 38

Îbrahîm, Ebdo, 116–18
India, 5
Iran, 35, 95, 100, 120
Iraq, 35–42 passim, 46, 89–90, 99, 120, 124; archaeological sites, 23; borders, 79, 86; Erbil, 50, 103, 134; Êzîdî, 14; Kurdancî, 6; Mosul, 129; refugees from, 100, 112; Tal Afar, 102–3; Turkmens, 102
Islam, 20. *See also* Shia Muslims; Sunni Muslims
Islamic Front, 74, 116
Islamic State (IS), 20, 65–69 passim, 74, 83–87 passim, 95, 97, 102–3, 114–18 passim, 127–29 passim
Islamic State in Iraq and Sham (ISIS), 65, 66, 74

Jabhat al-Akrad (Enîya Kurdan), 66, 68, 72, 114, 117
Jabhat al-Nusra, 13, 62, 65, 66, 74, 81n6, 114, 116
Jews, 20–21
Josef, Mesgin, 121–24

Justice and Development Party
(Turkey). *See* Adalet ve Kalkınma
Partisi (AKP)

Kamil Pasha al-Qudsi, 31–32
Karayılan, Murat, 48, 107
Karlow, Andrey, 70
KCK. *See* Koma Civakên Kurdistan
(KCK)
KÊRKS. *See* Komela Êzdiyên Rojavayê
Kurdistanê û Sûriye (KÊRKS)
Khalo, Mahmūd, 72, 79
Kilis, 1–2, 20, 21, 27–32 passim, 66, 69
King Feisal I. *See* Feisal I, King
Kneissl, Karin, 89
Kobanê (city), 47
Koma Civakên Kurdistan (KCK), 45
Komela Êzdiyên Rojavayê Kurdistanê
û Sûriye (KÊRKS), 15, 122, 133
"Kurd Dagh" (name), 1
Kurdish Democratic United Party
(Wifaq), 46
Kurdish Democratic Unity Party in
Syria (Yekîtî). *See* Partiya Yekîtî ya
Demokrat a Kurdî li Sûriyê (Yekîtî)
Kurdish Islamic Front, 65
Kurdish language, 4, 5, 37, 43; in
schools, 61, 125
Kurdish Left Party (Syria). *See* Partiya
Çep a Kurdî li Sûriyê (Kurdish
Leftist Party)
Kurdish National Alliance in Syria,
56
Kurdish National Council (ENKS),
39n46, 40n48, 49–56 passim, 79,
90–91, 110, 111, 118, 123–27 passim,
133
Kurdish Unity Party of Syria. *See*
Partiya Yekîtî ya Demokrat a Kurdî
li Sûriyê (Yekîtî)
Kurdistan Democratic Party (Iraq).
See Partiya Demokrat a Kurdistanê
(PDK)
Kuwait, 64, 123n1

Lališ (Lalish), Iraq, 120

land expropriation, 37
languages, 4–6, 16, 24, 28. *See also*
Arabic; Kurdish language
Lavrov, Sergey, 89
League of Nations, 31
Lebanon, 38–39, 43
Lekto, Fatme, 116
Lescot, Roger, 9, 14
Lîsta Netewa Demokratîk (LND), 55,
56
Liwa al-Tawhid, 66, 74, 75
Liwa Asifat al-Shamal. *See* Northern
Storm Brigade (Liwa Asifat
al-Shamal)

Mamluks, 28
Maron, Saint, 18
Maronites, 18
Mendî, 27–28, 29
military draft, 117–18
Mîllî, 31
Milliyetçi Hareket Partisi (MHP), 77,
133
Mithraism, 10
Mittani empire, 23
mosques, 8, 28, 84, 110
Movement for a Democratic Society.
See Tevgera Civaka Demokratîk
(TEV-DEM)
Muridin (Murûdan) movement,
33–34, 35
Muslim, Salih, 47, 89, 127–28
Muslim Brotherhood, 36, 65
Muslims, Shia. *See* Shia Muslims
Mustefa, Hêvî Îbrahîm, 17, 52, 54, 55,
113–15

Naqshbandīya, 8
National Bloc, 33
National Coalition of Syrian
Revolutionary and Oppositional
Forces, 91, 123, 124
National Defense Forces (Syria), 96
National Party (Syria), 36

nationalism: Arab, xvii, 32–37 passim,
43; Armenian, 33; Kurdish, 30–31,
33; Turkish, 77, 133
Nationalist Movement Party
(Turkey). *See* Milliyetçi Hareket
Partisi (MHP)
North Atlantic Treaty Organization
(NATO), 89, 105
Northern Storm Brigade (Liwa Asifat
al-Shamal), 66
Norway, 123n1
Nubl, 21, 60, 62, 68, 95, 109, 114, 117
Nusayrians. *See* Alevi and Alevism

Öcalan, Abdullah, 38–39, 43–45
passim, 49, 107
olives, 2, 3, 57, 60
Ottoman Empire, 1, 28–31, 32, 33n25

Partiya Çep a Kurdî li Sûriyê
(Kurdish Leftist Party), 39–40,
39n46, 55
Partiya Dêmokrat a Kurd li Sûriyê
(PDKS), 35, 36, 39, 40, 134
Partiya Dêmokrat a Kurdi li Sûriyê
(PDKS) (el-Partî), 39, 40, 53, 72, 91,
92
Partiya Demokrat a Kurdistanê
(PDK), 39n44, 42, 92, 126, 133–34
Partiya Karkerên Kurdistanê (PKK),
13–15 passim, 38–51 passim, 56, 70,
77, 79, 90, 106–7, 134; ENKS and, 91;
Kamal Sido on, 126; Mesgin Josef
on, 121, 122; Salih Muslim on, 128
Partiya Yekîtîya Demokrat (PYD),
13, 44–60 passim, 64, 65, 74,
89–92 passim, 121–29 passim,
134; Muridin movement and, 34;
relations with other parties, 39n46,
40n48; Russian relations, 70. *See
also* Movement for a Democratic
Society (TEV-DEM)
Partiya Yekîtîya Demokrat a Kurdî li
Sûriyê (Yekîtî), 40n48, 52–53, 55, 56
Partiya Yekîtîya Kurdî li Sûriyê. *See*
Kurdish Unity Party of Syria

Patriotic Union of Kurdistan (PUK),
39n45, 134
PDK. *See* Partiya Demokrat a
Kurdistanê (PDK)
PDKS. *See* Partiya Dêmokrat a Kurd li
Sûriyê (PDKS); Partiya Dêmokrat a
Kurdi li Sûriyê (PDKS) (el-Partî)
Peoples' Democratic Party (Turkey).
See Halkların Demokratik Partisi
(HDP)
People's Party (Syria), 36
People's Protection Forces. *See* Hêzên
Parastina Gel (HPG)
People's Protection Units. *See*
Yekîneyên Parastina Gel (YPG)
PFLP. *See* Popular Front for the
Liberation of Palestine (PFLP)
Pinto, Pablo, 9
PKK. *See* Partiya Karkerên
Kurdistanê (PKK)
plunder, xiv, 110
police, 21, 34, 42, 47–48, 59, 70, 116
Popular Front for the Liberation of
Palestine (PFLP), 38
propaganda, xv, 83–86 passim, 96–97,
101
protests and demonstrations. *See*
demonstrations
PUK. *See* Patriotic Union of
Kurdistan (PUK)
Putin, Vladimir, 80
PYD. *See* Partiya Yekîtîya Demokrat
(PYD)

Qādirīya, 8–9
Qamişlo, 20, 40, 42, 44, 46, 48, 110, 123;
universities, 61
Qatar, 64, 110, 121

Reco (city), 6, 19, 95
Red Crescent, 108
Red Cross, German. *See* Deutsch
Rotes Kreuz (German Red Cross)
refugees, xiv–xvii passim, 62–63, 75,
78, 95, 99–12 passim, 122; Arab, 3,

37; Armenian, 18, 32–33; EU policy,
    99–100; Kurdish, 17, 21, 33, 108
religion, 7–21
remittances, international (hawala),
    58–59
Republic of Hatay, 34
Republican People's Party (Turkey).
    See Cumhuriyet Halk Partisi (CHP)
Resistance Units of Şingal. See
    Yekîneyên Berxwedana Şengalê
    (YBŞ)
Robariya, 10
Roj Peshmerga, 91
Roma, 5, 41, 126
Roman Empire, 25
Rubari, 29, 30
Russia, xv, 70–71, 78–83 passim, 89, 94,
    105, 109; U.S. relations, 79–80

Saladin, 26–27
Sama, Schluwa, 98–99
Saudi Arabia, 64, 65
Savelsberg, Eva, 79
schooling. See education
SDF. See Syrian Democratic Forces
    (SDF)
Seleucids, 25, 27
Şêxmeqsûd (Sheikh Maqsood), 6, 74,
    75, 81
Shabo, Azad, 73, 74
Shafi'i school of law, 7
Shia Muslims, 16, 21, 66, 68, 103;
    militias, 94, 95, 96, 117
shrines, 14, 17
Sido, Kamal, 91, 124–27
Simon Stylites the Elder, 18
Şindi, Hasan, 110
Siyaset, Ekonomi ve Toplum
    Araştırmaları Vakfı (SETA), 91
Socialist-Nationalist Party. See Syrian
    Socialist-Nationalist Party
Socialist Party of Austria (SPÖ),
    45n55
Society for Threatened Peoples
    (Germany), 91, 127

Southeastern Anatolian Project. See
    Güneydoğu Anadolu Projesi (GAP)
Soviet Union, 43, 51–52
State of Syria, 32, 33
Sufi brotherhoods, 8–9
Sunni Muslims, 7, 16, 17, 18, 68, 110, 126;
    Turkmens, 102, 103
Supreme Kurdish Committee, 50
Syria (state). See Syrian State
Syrian Communist Party. See
    Communist Party of Syria
Syrian Democratic Forces (SDF),
    24, 68–71 passim, 75, 80, 89, 95;
    casualties, 106; fatwa against, 88
Syrian Federation (French
    protectorate era), 32
Syrian Islamic Council, 87–88
Syrian Islamic Front, 65
Syrian Islamic Liberation Front, 65
Syrian National Democratic Alliance,
    55, 56
Syrian National Party. See National
    Party (Syria)
Syrian Socialist-Nationalist Party, 36

Tal Afar, 102–3
Tal Aran. See Til Eren (Tal Aran)
Tal Rifaat, 24, 53, 54, 69, 108, 109, 129
"terrorist" (label), 44–45, 70, 78, 83–85
    passim, 95–97 passim, 131
Tevgera Civaka Demokratîk (TEV-
    DEM), 83, 127, 134
Teyrêbazên Efrînê. See Efrîn Falcons
Til Eren (Tal Aran), 6, 73
Turkey, xiv–xv, 1–3, 33–43 passim, 64;
    archaeological site destruction, 24;
    army, xiv, 19–20, 69, 80–87 passim,
    92–102 passim, 106–12 passim,
    129–31 passim; borders, 37, 66, 67,
    68, 69, 114–16 passim; economic
    blockade, 114; EU relations, xv,
    99–100; Muridin movement, 33;
    Öcalan, 43; occupation of Afrin,
    xiv, 93, 108–12 passim, 130; Russian
    relations, 70–71, 78, 81, 89; U.S.
    relations, 68; war against Afrin,

xiv, 13, 19-24 passim, 56, 77-112. *See also* Antakya, Turkey; Kilis
Turkish Doctors' Association, 85
Turkmenization, xv, 78, 102-5 passim, 112
Turkmens, 102-3, 111

Union of the Communities of Kurdistan. *See* Koma Civakên Kurdistan (KCK)
Union of the Êzîdî of Syria (Hevbendiya Êzîdiyên Suriyê). *See* Hevbendiya Êzîdiyên Suriyê (HÊS)
United Arab Republic, 36
United Kingdom, 123n1. *See also* British in Syria
United Nations, 45n55, 94
United States, 44-45, 46, 68-71 passim, 81, 83, 88, 89, 90; CIA, 35; Russian relations, 79-80
universities, 61-62
USSR. *See* Soviet Union

water supply, 58, 105
women, xi-xii, 41, 113, 116; cooperatives, 59-60; police, 59, 116; quotas in government, 50, 51, 116; sexual violence, 63
Women's Protection Units. *See* Yekîneyên Parastina Jin (YPJ)
Women's Units of Êzidxan. *See* Yekinêyen Jinên Êzidxan (YJÊ)
Workers' Party of Kurdistan. *See* Partiya Karkerên Kurdistanê (PKK)
World War II, 34-35

Xelîl, Rêdûr, 48, 69
Xoybûn, 33

Yarsanism, 10
Yekîneyên Berxwedana Şengalê (YBŞ), 93, 134
Yekinêyen Jinên Êzidxan (YJÊ), 93, 134
Yekîneyên Parastina Gel (YPG), xiv, 52, 66-83 passim, 88-97 passim,

104n42, 106-17 passim, 121, 129-34 passim; border control, 13, 66-67; founding, 48; Germany, 45n55
Yekîneyên Parastina Jin (YPJ), xi-xiv passim, 67-69 passim, 75-83 passim, 82, 92-97 passim, 117, 121, 130, 132, 134; border control, 13, 66-67; Fatme Lekto on, 116; founding, 48
Yekîtî. *See* Partiya Yekîtî ya Demokrat a Kurdî li Sûriyê (Yekîtî)
Yezidis. *See* Êzîdî
Yıldırım, Binali, 83
YPG. *See* Yekîneyên Parastina Gel (YPG)
YPJ. *See* Yekîneyên Parastina Jin (YPJ)

Zengids, 26
Zoroastrianism, 10, 13, 14, 119-20

About the Authors

Thomas Schmidinger is political scientist at the University of Vienna, secretary general of the Austrian Association for Kurdish Studies, and coeditor of the *Vienna Kurdish Studies Yearbook*. He is in the board of the NGO LeEZA and writes on Kurdistan, Iraq, Syria, Sudan, Kosovo, political Islam, jihadism, and migration. His previous book *Rojava: Revolution, War and the Future of Syria's Kurds* (2018) was awarded the Mazlum Bagok prize.

Andrej Grubačić is the chair of the Anthropology and Social Change department at the California Institute of Integral Studies. His books include *Don't Mourn, Balkanize: Essays after Yugoslavia*. Andrej is a member of the International Council of the World Social Forum, the Industrial Workers of the World, and the Global Balkans Network.

Michael Schiffmann is a linguist, cultural scientist, translator, editor, and author and teaches at the Universities of Heidelberg and Mannheim. He is working on a research project on the history of Noam Chomsky's generative grammar and is active in the international campaigns to free Mumia Abu-Jamal and Leonard Peltier. As well as Schmidinger's previous book, *Rojava: Revolution, War, and the Future of Syria's Kurds*, he has translated works by Mumia Abu-Jamal, Homi K. Bhabha, Noam Chomsky, Mahmoud Darwish, Angela Davis, Amy Goodman, Ilan Pappé, Miko Peled, and Edward Said.

ABOUT PM PRESS

PM Press was founded at the end of 2007 by a small collection of folks with decades of publishing, media, and organizing experience. PM Press co-conspirators have published and distributed hundreds of books, pamphlets, CDs, and DVDs. Members of PM have founded enduring book fairs, spearheaded victorious tenant organizing campaigns, and worked closely with bookstores, academic conferences, and even rock bands to deliver political and challenging ideas to all walks of life. We're old enough to know what we're doing and young enough to know what's at stake.

We seek to create radical and stimulating fiction and nonfiction books, pamphlets, T-shirts, visual and audio materials to entertain, educate, and inspire you. We aim to distribute these through every available channel with every available technology—whether that means you are seeing anarchist classics at our bookfair stalls, reading our latest vegan cookbook at the café, downloading geeky fiction e-books, or digging new music and timely videos from our website.

PM Press is always on the lookout for talented and skilled volunteers, artists, activists, and writers to work with. If you have a great idea for a project or can contribute in some way, please get in touch.

PM Press
PO Box 23912
Oakland, CA 94623
www.pmpress.org

PM Press in Europe
europe@pmpress.org
www.pmpress.org.uk

FRIENDS OF PM PRESS

These are indisputably momentous times—the financial system is melting down globally and the Empire is stumbling. Now more than ever there is a vital need for radical ideas.

In the years since its founding—and on a mere shoestring—PM Press has risen to the formidable challenge of publishing and distributing knowledge and entertainment for the struggles ahead. With over 300 releases to date, we have published an impressive and stimulating array of literature, art, music, politics, and culture. Using every available medium, we've succeeded in connecting those hungry for ideas and information to those putting them into practice.

Friends of PM allows you to directly help impact, amplify, and revitalize the discourse and actions of radical writers, filmmakers, and artists. It provides us with a stable foundation from which we can build upon our early successes and provides a much-needed subsidy for the materials that can't necessarily pay their own way. You can help make that happen—and receive every new title automatically delivered to your door once a month—by joining as a Friend of PM Press. And, we'll throw in a free T-shirt when you sign up.

Here are your options:

- **$30 a month** Get all books and pamphlets plus 50% discount on all webstore purchases

- **$40 a month** Get all PM Press releases (including CDs and DVDs) plus 50% discount on all webstore purchases

- **$100 a month** Superstar—Everything plus PM merchandise, free downloads, and 50% discount on all webstore purchases

For those who can't afford $30 or more a month, we have **Sustainer Rates** at $15, $10 and $5. Sustainers get a free PM Press T-shirt and a 50% discount on all purchases from our website.

Your Visa or Mastercard will be billed once a month, until you tell us to stop. Or until our efforts succeed in bringing the revolution around. Or the financial meltdown of Capital makes plastic redundant. Whichever comes first.

DEPARTMENT OF ANTHROPOLOGY & SOCIAL CHANGE

Anthropology and Social Change, housed within
the California Institute of Integral Studies, is a small
innovative graduate department with a particular focus
on activist scholarship, militant research, and social change. We offer both masters
and doctoral degree programs.

Our unique approach to collaborative research methodology dissolves traditional
barriers between research and political activism, between insiders and outsiders,
and between researchers and protagonists. Activist research is a tool for "creating
the conditions we describe." We engage in the process of co-research to explore
existing alternatives and possibilities for social change.

Anthropology and Social Change
anth@ciis.edu
1453 Mission Street
94103
San Francisco, California
www.ciis.edu/academics/graduate-programs/anthropology-and-social-change

We Are the Crisis of Capital: A John Holloway Reader

John Holloway

ISBN: 978-1-62963-225-4
$22.95   320 pages

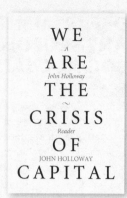

We Are the Crisis of Capital collects articles and excerpts written by radical academic, theorist, and activist John Holloway over a period of forty years.

Different times, different places, and the same anguish persists throughout our societies. This collection asks, "Is there a way out?" How do we break capital, a form of social organisation that dehumanises us and threatens to annihilate us completely? How do we create a world based on the mutual recognition of human dignity?

Holloway's work answers loudly, "By screaming NO!" By thinking from our own anger and from our own creativity. By trying to recover the "We" who are buried under the categories of capitalist thought. By opening the categories and discovering the antagonism they conceal, by discovering that behind the concepts of money, state, capital, crisis, and so on, there moves our resistance and rebellion.

An approach sometimes referred to as Open Marxism, it is an attempt to rethink Marxism as daily struggle. The articles move forward, influenced by the German state derivation debates of the seventies, by the CSE debates in Britain, and the group around the Edinburgh journal *Common Sense*, and then moving on to Mexico and the wonderful stimulus of the Zapatista uprising, and now the continuing whirl of discussion with colleagues and students in the Posgrado de Sociología of the Benemérita Universidad Autónoma de Puebla.

"Holloway's work is infectiously optimistic."
—Steven Poole, the *Guardian* (UK)

"Holloway's thesis is indeed important and worthy of notice."
—Richard J.F. Day, *Canadian Journal of Cultural Studies*

Re-enchanting the World: Feminism and the Politics of the Commons

Silvia Federici
with a Foreword by Peter Linebaugh

ISBN: 978-1-62963-569-9
$19.95   240 pages

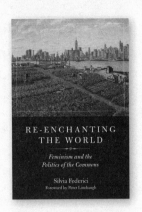

Silvia Federici is one of the most important contemporary theorists of capitalism and feminist movements. In this collection of her work spanning over twenty years, she provides a detailed history and critique of the politics of the commons from a feminist perspective. In her clear and combative voice, Federici provides readers with an analysis of some of the key issues and debates in contemporary thinking on this subject.

Drawing on rich historical research, she maps the connections between the previous forms of enclosure that occurred with the birth of capitalism and the destruction of the commons and the "new enclosures" at the heart of the present phase of global capitalist accumulation. Considering the commons from a feminist perspective, this collection centers on women and reproductive work as crucial to both our economic survival and the construction of a world free from the hierarchies and divisions capital has planted in the body of the world proletariat. Federici is clear that the commons should not be understood as happy islands in a sea of exploitative relations but rather autonomous spaces from which to challenge the existing capitalist organization of life and labor.

"*Silvia Federici's theoretical capacity to articulate the plurality that fuels the contemporary movement of women in struggle provides a true toolbox for building bridges between different features and different people.*"
—Massimo De Angelis, professor of political economy, University of East London

"*Silvia Federici's work embodies an energy that urges us to rejuvenate struggles against all types of exploitation and, precisely for that reason, her work produces a common: a common sense of the dissidence that creates a community in struggle.*"
—Maria Mies, coauthor of *Ecofeminism*

Don't Mourn, Balkanize!
Essays After Yugoslavia

Andrej Grubačić with an introduction by
Roxanne Dunbar-Ortiz

ISBN: 978-1-60486-302-4
$20.00   272 pages

Don't Mourn, Balkanize! is the first book written from the
radical left perspective on the topic of Yugoslav space
after the dismantling of the country. In this collection of
essays, commentaries and interviews, written between
2002 and 2010, Andrej Grubačić speaks about the politics of balkanization—
about the trial of Slobodan Milošević, the assassination of Prime Minister Zoran
Djindjic, neoliberal structural adjustment, humanitarian intervention, supervised
independence of Kosovo, occupation of Bosnia, and other episodes of Power which
he situates in the long historical context of colonialism, conquest and intervention.

But he also tells the story of the balkanization of politics, of the Balkans seen from
below. A space of bogumils—those medieval heretics who fought against Crusades
and churches—and a place of anti-Ottoman resistance; a home to hajduks and
klefti, pirates and rebels; a refuge of feminists and socialists, of anti-fascists
and partisans; of new social movements of occupied and recovered factories; a
place of dreamers of all sorts struggling both against provincial "peninsularity"
as well as against occupations, foreign interventions and that process which is
now, in a strange inversion of history, often described by that fashionable term,
"balkanization."

For Grubačić, political activist and radical sociologist, Yugoslavia was never just
a country—it was an idea. Like the Balkans itself, it was a project of inter-ethnic
co-existence, a trans-ethnic and pluricultural space of many diverse worlds.
Political ideas of inter-ethnic cooperation and mutual aid as we had known them
in Yugoslavia were destroyed by the beginning of the 1990s—disappeared in the
combined madness of ethno-nationalist hysteria and humanitarian imperialism.
This remarkable collection chronicles political experiences of the author who is
himself a Yugoslav, a man without a country; but also, as an anarchist, a man
without a state. This book is an important reading for those on the Left who are
struggling to understand the intertwined legacy of inter-ethnic conflict and inter-
ethnic solidarity in contemporary, post-Yugoslav history.

*"These thoughtful essays offer us a vivid picture of the Balkans experience from the
inside, with its richness and complexity, tragedy and hope, and lessons from which we
can all draw inspiration and insight."*
—Noam Chomsky